mini mini me:

a guide to a minimalist life

lily ennis

About the Author

Lily lives near Thames, New Zealand with three moggies, a middle aged cockatoo she inherited from her grandmother, and her husband. She has a Bachelor of Business Studies (VPM) and a Bachelor of Science (Earth Science). After decades of tramping the New Zealand bush she has discovered the joys of bike touring. When she isn't plotting another book she can be found singing in the local choir. She has practiced minimalism since being tasked with clearing her grandmother's house some years ago.

For Olina

without whom the idea for this book

may never have been realised

Other titles by Lily Ennis

Fire in the Mountain, 2012

Seaton's War, 2013

Scarlet Runner, 2014

Blue Rider, 2016

The Ballot Farm, 2019

Earthflight One: A Dragon's Adventure, 2013

Earthflight Two: Dragon's Quest, 2014

Notes

The goal of this book is to introduce the reader to the philosophy of living mindfully. It is not a scientific paper. I have therefore limited the references. This demonstrates that I'm not making stuff up. I encourage the reader to do his or her own research. There are many scientific concepts which are necessary for the reader to have some understanding of and I have tried to explain these in a way that is comprehensible to the reader. Where possible I have drawn diagrams. These concepts are academically accepted principles and no references are attached to these.

Table of Contents

INTRODUCTION

"It is preoccupation with possessions more than anything else that prevents men from living freely and nobly." Bertrand Russell 1872, Founder of Analytical Philosophy, Logician, Utilitarianist, Nobel Prize winner in Literature.

I am a minimalist. But not like Gandhi who is said to have had only ten possessions when he died. As a working woman I need a bit more than a robe, bowl and spoon, sandals, spectacles, a watch and a couple of books. Besides, where I come from it is freezing in winter. It simply isn't practical to get by with a robe. My clothes are an expression of who I am and being minimalist does not mean being boring although I concede there is a wardrobe ethic that some minimalists subscribe to that leaves me cold. I extend my minimalist philosophy to how I purchase my clothes, from ethical considerations to the look I want to achieve.

I wrote this book as a response to a throwaway line by a friend who suggested I do so. I had commented on her husband's garage, crammed with a project car that he admitted he was never going to get around to starting let alone finishing. She then mentioned trawling through her mother's things as her mother had died recently and that one room in the house was now dedicated to that painful task. I remarked that I'd been there and done that and by the end of the process I'd become a minimalist and now embraced the philosophy fully. I embrace walking lightly on the planet.

Writing the book led me to analyse the decisions I make around purchasing. The experience written about is my own. When I put into words the minimalist philosophy as to how it relates to me, the subject grew bigger than I imagined. But I make no apology for such wordy articulation. For one thing you will come to understand as you make your way through the book is that all actions have consequences. Minimalism tends to make me consider the consequences of making a purchase before I make that purchase. Am I harming any person or the planet by my purchase? When I need to dispose of the item, likewise, am I causing harm? In order to fully embrace the practice it is necessary to understand how our actions have consequences. Otherwise you don't know why you're doing it and it becomes impossible to adhere to principles if you don't understand them.

What then, is minimalism? Various dictionary definitions characterise minimalism as a style dominated by extreme sparseness and simplicity. The Cambridge English Dictionary has it relating to a style in art, design and theatre that uses the smallest range of materials and colours possible, and only very simple shapes or forms.

In a nutshell that is the essence of what minimalism is. What the definition shies clear of is what minimalism is actually about. Why would anybody choose less over more? What is the point in using restricted colours, materials, forms? Surely minimalism is a western fad. There are hundreds of blogs and books on the subject, the majority by practitioners in wealthy countries.

In this book I attempt to prove that minimalism is not a western fad. Nor is it particularly new. Many cultures around the world live a minimalist lifestyle. We explore this in chapter one; culture.

My experience is that of a white woman living in a western society. That is my culture. This is the cultural background that I bring to this book. You need to know this, if you are going to understand my perception of minimalism. My perception of course is mine, just as yours is yours. I am a child of a consumerist society. I was born in the sixties, the last of the baby boomers to wear home knitted clothes and use cloth nappies. Soon however, new and exciting innovations became commonplace: television, international travel, disposable nappies and plastic. The world has shrunk considerably since I was born and it has rapidly become a consumerist, throwaway society.

You may be just like me, wrestling with the constant bombardment of advertisers trying to sell me junk so I can feel happy, or dealing with the guilt of discarding unwanted gifts, and clinging onto inherited antiques because that is what is expected of me. Perhaps you just go with the flow. You know what the latest fad is, know where to go to get the bargains, can sing all the advertising jingles. Are you even conscious that you know all this stuff?

My home environment is as serene as I can possibly make it. It isn't easy in this day and age, with marketers constantly in my face. One tactic I use is to ban junk mail. It does not make it inside the front door, because there is nothing, not a bean nor a brass razoo, that I want to buy. You probably asked why I don't have a "No Junk Mail" sticker on my letterbox. My husband loves junk mail so it's literally a race to the box. If I get there first I just hide it in my car until it's safe to dump it into the recycle bin, without reading it of course.

To embrace minimalism is to love clean surfaces, to embrace the void. Dust collectors have no place in the minimalist home. Ornaments go to opportunity shops or to friends. Stuff does not accumulate. No more cute little storage boxes to store small stuff. No more big storage units on the other side of town to store big stuff.

In this book I talk a lot about "stuff". It is a great word which encompasses everything from the smallest knickknacks to the bulkiest furniture. Stuff can be useful or completely useless. Have a look around your room right now. There is a lot of stuff isn't there? Stuff sneaks up on a person. Watch a friend move into a new home, a bigger one than they previously had, and watch how stuff infiltrates that house over the course of only one year. They don't even notice it happening. I say to watch a friend because it's easy to observe from a distance. It will have happened to you but you will not have noticed. Stuff is so sneaky you don't even notice when it sneaks up on you. In this book stuff is our enemy. I like to think of stuff like this:

S - Surplus

T - Thingamajigs are

U - Unnecessary for living

F- Fuss

F - Free

Before you start your minimalist journey you need to know why you're doing it. Perhaps you're fed up with the whole consumer thing. You are sick of every one of your senses being bombarded with insidious advertising urging you to spend your hard earned money on shiny new gadgets which apparently guarantee happiness. It could be that you just can't get from one side of the room to the other without tripping over stuff. The beauty of space has somehow bypassed you.

It can be overwhelming to start throwing stuff out. In chapter two we talk about the freedom that results when your stuff isn't controlling you. All that clutter is preventing you from thinking clearly. It's easy to feel comfortably uncomfortable in a house full of stuff. You constantly move piles of junk from one spot to another while looking for something. That could be your tidying up style. But if this is your style you are not in control. Your possessions are controlling you.

This isn't one of those books that challenge you to pare down your wardrobe to thirty items, or to throw out one thing each day. There are hundreds of blogs out there for that. This is about getting your life back from the hold your possessions have on you. This is about regaining control and enjoying the freedom that ensues. On the way we will explore the philosophy of living minimally through glimpses into its application in the arts and environmentalism, even in how you eat.

The book is loosely organised into the personal view and the world view. The two are intertwined since you become aware of how your personal actions impact the world. I present environmentalism as a world view and you will quickly see how a small purchase of stuff by you has consequences for the planet. If after reading this book you are disturbed at what is happening then minimalism is for you. It is all the easier to adhere to the practice because you understand the consequences of not doing so.

There are a lot of questions you ask of your possessions when you begin the minimalist journey:

- Why am I keeping you?

- Do I really need two, three, four of you?

- Whatever possessed me to buy you?

- What am I going to do with you?

And the exclamations when you finally open that box in the bottom of the wardrobe:

- Gosh I'd forgotten I had that!

- I wondered where that was!

- I used to love this!

Now guess what? Because you haven't looked in the box for years, you sure as heck don't need what's in there. Chances are you've kept the stuff because it has sentimental value. And that's half the problem with stuff. It carries so much emotional baggage. We'll deal with the emotional side of selling your inheritance in Chapter 11 when we get down to the nuts and bolts of decluttering.

I'm going to show you how to declutter each room, each drawer and cupboard. Then I'll suggest how you can continue the practice so stuff doesn't sneak up on you again.

But don't think it stops there. It simply marks the first step in becoming a minimalist. It's a long philosophical journey that seeps into every aspect of your life. For instance you become aware of the whole concept of minimalism in how the built environment looks and thus enhances or upsets your feelings towards it. For instance, think of a Japanese Zen garden with three carefully placed rocks on a ground of raked sand. Likely you will feel calm. Your eyes are drawn to the shape of the rocks, the textures and any imperfections on the surfaces. You study the rhythm of the lines in the sand. Each element, not competing for space, has your attention. Even the space has your attention.

Contrast this with the hustle and bustle of a rambling English country garden in full summer. You literally don't know where to look first. It's like being a kid in a candy store. Not that there is anything wrong with an English country garden, for it is a beautiful thing with butterflies and bees and a breeze to rustle the leaves and whisk the petals from the flowers. There is always something going on, something new to look at. The point I make is the difference in the feeling that you get from the two contrasting experiences.

Chapter 6 looks at minimalism in the visual arts and you might be surprised to learn that minimalism is far from a new idea. The various art movements show that minimalism is hard won. Artists are famous for rebelling against the establishment. It doesn't matter what style has gone before, it is doomed to be railed against by the new guard.

To illustrate that point that the minimalist ethos is not new I have chosen quotes from notable people down through the ages to place at each chapter heading. What is interesting is that many of the proponents of the simple life were themselves born into privilege but their humility saw them shun possessions as a path to spiritual wealth.

As I sit here on a hot summer's day under a silk tree, in the garden, I notice a sparrows' nest fallen out of a tree. How a tiny bird can make such a perfect nest with only its beak is a wonder to behold. It is a perfect half globe. The interior is not scratchy with leaves and sticks and bits of grass as the exterior is, rather, it is cemented smooth to make the structure strong and comfortable for the chicks. The chicks have fledged, the parents flown away too. The temporary home has done its job.

Welcome to the Tiny House Movement. Environmentally responsible, tiny house dwellers are the epitome of minimalism. They have little worry for housework and more time for the important things – experiencing life on this amazing planet, volunteering, spending time with friends and family.

For some people simplifying life can mean simplifying their diet. These days that doesn't mean eating rice from one small bowl like Gandhi, but if clearing one's mind and embracing environmentalism are natural flow on effects of minimalism, then it can extend to how we eat. In the west we eat what we want when we want. In this shrinking world we have come to expect to be able to obtain any food products we desire at any time of the year. Gone are the days of pickling and bottling summer fruit for eating during the year. Food is simply flown in from overseas.

Meat, milk, eggs: staples in many households. But how many children in this urban world associate those products with the animals they came from? How many parents understand that it takes one thousand litres of water to produce one litre of milk? Chapter 10 discusses the environmental effects of purchasing and eating out of season food as well as the effects of eating meat and dairy products.

I am vegan for reasons of animal ethics. I don't need to eat animals to keep me alive. I don't want them kept in paddocks or cages just to give me milk or eggs. The alternative to the traditional western diet is astoundingly delicious. And what's really great is that having embraced environmentalism as a natural effect of minimalism, the foray into veganism takes you into a beautiful world of whole foods, no packaging and ethical purchasing.

It isn't hard to be vegan when you know why you are doing it. Vegans generally eschew the harming of life, any life. However, lately veganism is seen as a poster child to save the planet. And in my book that isn't bad. There certainly is a movement whereby people are choosing to eat a more plant-based diet in order to save the planet. As long as you understand why you are doing something it becomes pretty easy to stick to.

We also explore how we purchase goods. Or rather, how the corporations have us purchase goods. In Chapter 3 we consider the difference between needs and wants. It might be obvious to you, or you might never have had the opportunity to think about it before. I want to give you the opportunity to use the concept of needs versus wants when it comes to de-cluttering.

In Chapter 5 we discuss social conscience as it relates to your purchasing power. This chapter illustrates beautifully how a small ethical purchase made by you can have positive consequences for a worker on the other side of the planet.

You didn't expect all that from a little browse into minimalism did you?

As outlined above we are going to explore a new attitude to possessions. To help with this transition, the rearranging of your thoughts and your attitude to stuff, I'm going to talk about setting things free when you need to part with something. You don't want to be grieving over parting with stuff. It should be a joyous liberation. When you set it free, or pass it on, it will find a new home and a new lease of life. In fact, if your local opportunity shop is your preferred recipient then someone will pay good money for your stuff, which in turn supports your cause. That's got to make you feel great.

At the end of each chapter I present practical ideas that you may implement on your journey towards minimalism. It does take a little time to confidently announce to friends and family that you are a minimalist but by the time you have got to that stage you will have a deep sense of joy.

1

CULTURE

"Joy comes not through possession or ownership but through a wise and loving heart." Siddhartha Gautama, Founder of Buddhism.

It's not easy to define one's own culture. It's like trying to describe yourself. You can't see the wood for the trees. Someone else, however, can make observations through the benefit of distance. Culture can be defined as the norms and traditions of a society. These comprise the rites of passage: the way we enter the world, how we are treated as children, adults, men or women, our inclusion in groups, the ceremonies we take part in and how we deal with our dead.

The way we make art or music, and how we build cities is a reflection of the values of the society to which we belong. Look around your own house. Notice how many objects are crammed onto the mantelpiece, the sideboard, the dining room table. I think you can agree with me that a cultural tradition of western society is that of consumption.

Below I include a brief introduction into cultures that demonstrate minimalism as a way of life. As a lifestyle it is practiced consciously in the case of Zen Buddhism and perhaps less consciously but for entirely different reasons in the case of nomadic peoples. I introduce these only to broaden our views on what we think minimalism is. As always, there is something to learn from other people.

Ma - the principle of emptiness

Try now to imagine the interior of a Japanese house. You probably have never been inside one but you will have a preconception of clean lines, no clutter and a feeling of restful space. This is what the Japanese refer to as Ma.

Ma is pervasive in Japanese life. It is a love of emptiness, with emphasis on negative space. The void between objects has equal importance to the objects themselves. This is quite the opposite point of view to Picasso who famously stated "I don't paint what I see, but what I know" in explaining why he painted both a side view and a front view in the one portrait. His style left nothing to the viewer's imagination. Where is the ma, the emptiness full of unfilled promise?

This concept isn't only found inside the Japanese home. It is found in architecture, garden design, music and flower arrangements. Ma has its foundations in Zen Buddhism. Zen means meditation in Japanese. The meditation practice is to experience living in the present through releasing your mind and your consciousness to merge with the universe. Zen places emphasis on simplicity as a way to achieve inner freedom. This principle is known as Wabi-sabi and it is concerned with finding value in simple forms of nature.

Seijaku, or stillness, is another principle of Zen meditation, the state being achieved through simple design concepts such as tranquillity, harmony and balance.

These things define the culture of the Japanese. It is not hard to understand how the ancient Buddhist tradition impacts on Japanese culture. This highly technological nation has deep roots in minimalist philosophy.

Nomads

Many people across the globe live a transient lifestyle, from the Arctic Circle, to the Mongolian Steppe to Saharan Africa. Common to these peoples is their special relationship with the land and to the animals on it. As animal farmers, they move according to the availability of food. Mongolian herders winter near a mountain for the shelter it affords. In spring they park up close to a river. Summer sees the group camp on the banks of a river and in autumn they will go up a hill to collect hay for the winter. Each of these locations forms part of the regular circuit. They know where they are going and for how long.

The fact that they move house, or ger, several times throughout the year suggests they also have a different relationship with their possessions than Westerners might. Inside a ger there are couches draped in rugs, cupboards, a table, a woodstove, television and fridge. Photographs adorn the walls. There is nothing impermanent about a nomad's home. However, as everything is carried by horse it does mean the ability to accumulate superfluous stuff is limited.

Inuit reindeer herders of the Arctic Circle live a life of migration as they swap eight months of winter for summer pastures on which their reindeer can graze. Reindeer sustain these people providing food, clothing and shelter. However, reindeer are revered, no matter how they are used. According to the Inuit, the reindeer and humans enter a social contract. The reindeer offer themselves to humans for their subsistence and transport and humans agree to accompany them on their seasonal migrations to protect them from predators.

Unfortunately beneath the tundra are large gas deposits. The consumer culture of the rest of the world is a threat to this ancient way of life.

Worldwide there are thousands of traditional societies. Communities that have survived and thrived for thousands of years have, in little over one hundred years, become accessible to the Western world, with our motor cars, computers and mobile phones. Motor cycles replace horses and ski-doos replace dog sleds. It makes life easier doesn't it? This contact has irreversibly changed nomadic societies. Cultures not normally associated with technology are exposed to the consumerist excesses of Western society. Of course people want new technology. But does it lead to being swallowed by the consumer treadmill of work to pay debt?Does owning more stuff make any of us truly happy?

2

FREEDOM

"If one's life is simple, contentment has to come. Simplicity is extremely important for happiness. Having few desires, feeling satisfied with what you have, is very vital." Dalai Lama (b. 1935)

The Consumer Machine

Freedom of choice or freedom from choice? It is indisputable that we have the freedom to choose whatever we want to buy. We can decide we want to buy something, perhaps because we saw an advertisement, then make enquiries as to the best product to suit our purpose. There are many considerations to make: price, colour, brand, availability, method of delivery, financing, fashion, the eventual disposal of the item, depreciation and image, to name a few.

Barry Schwartz[1] suggests that material affluence is a problem peculiar to modern western society. Has the freedom of choice become our nemesis? Look at the length companies go to in order to sell us something. There is advertising in print, television, social media and radio, branding in the form of attaching a company name to a sports team and marketing gurus who position a brand into a preferred price stream and demographic. Careers are made on clever sales campaigns.

There is the limited time special price, the two for one special price, the loyalty card, the loyalty card where points can be transferred to another company's loyalty card, the lucky shopper, VIP cardholder nights, the clearance sale, summer sale, winter sale, stock-take sale, Easter sale, Christmas sale, Waitangi Day sale, back to school sale, Black Tuesday, Mother's Day sale, Father's Day sale. There are just as many ways to purchase the must have items while they're on offer at heavily discounted prices. There is buy now pay later, the revolving mortgage, and that's where they use the term "put it on the house" interest free for thirty six months (store financing), credit card, debit card, or even cash. Try using cash and I bet the urge to own that "never again at this price" item well and truly passes.

How many ways can rice be sold to wealthy westerners? Quite a lot apparently. It's the staple food of billions of people but in the west we need to add value to it by presenting it in a small attractive plastic bag in a supermarket. It's a bit like thinking of the humble spud being sold in trays of two. At the end of the day rice is rice and potatoes are potatoes. But ticket clippers along the way would have us believe that their rice is best or their potatoes are choicest. This adds value to the product, thereby contributing to the economic wellbeing of supply chain workers, but creating a decision dilemma for the shopper.

I'm not advocating the alternative. To have choice is to exercise freedom. I'm simply pointing out that we are ensconced in a phenomenon never seen before in history. We can have anything we want these days thanks to global trade and advertising makes us aware of that. We can have so much of what we fancy that we just buy it because it is cheap and buying stuff makes us feel good. Hopefully by the time you finish reading this book the thought of buying stuff will make you feel ill.

Let's do a simple thought experiment. Try to imagine walking into a house cluttered with memorabilia, dust collectors, "to do" piles. Magazines and newspapers are stacked on the table tops, on the floor, tucked into a corner. Dust bunnies gather at the edges of the piles. A load of firewood sits on the hearth, bits of bark and sawdust litter the ground. On the mantelpiece is every knick knack that you've collected in the last five years and not known what to do with. On the kitchen bench sits a row of gadgets that get used every couple of months, if that. The fridge is covered with kitchen magnets. This could be your house.

How does that make you feel? Did your heart race? Did your brow furrow, your teeth clench and your shoulders tense? I know those things happened to you.

Now picture yourself standing in a major art gallery. It is early. There are no crowds. You stand in the centre of the room. Visualise the highly polished wooden floor. Observe the way it feels beneath your feet. Notice the white walls. There is one painting on a wall, a simple statue on a white plinth in the centre of the room and an iron bench for you to rest on while you contemplate the experience.

You had a completely different reaction didn't you? A sense of calm washed over you. Wouldn't you like this feeling every day? I know I would.

In my experience when I visit friends in their cluttered houses my eyes are too quickly diverted from my friend to everything else that's jammed inside the house. It's just plain hard to concentrate on my friend. It feels like I'm being swallowed by the house. To the outsider it looks like junk but to your friend it's all meaningful. The inhabitants clearly have lost control.

Consumer culture demands that we treat ourselves. The popular psychology of today is to just do it. Just buy it and to hang with the consequences. Buy now pay later. What that means is it doesn't matter if you think you can't afford it. They will make you believe you can afford it. They will lock you into an exorbitant interest rate which you will agree to pay out of your future earnings. You'll feel great, after all, self-indulgence is good for you, whereas frugality is self-oppression and old fashioned.

When did it happen that what we own defines us? Is it a function of living in an industrialised society? Or does the concept date back to the middle ages, the bronze age or the stone age? I suggest that the practice of conveying rank or regency by the clothes worn and the adornments that go with them is as old as human society. Perhaps we can understand a Pasifika woman of nobility wearing the most intricately carved rare shell comb while lesser women wear common shell combs, not so elaborately carved. Through the ages items were hand-made and revered for all the work that went into making them.

Craftsmen were commissioned. Their skill was recognised and rewarded. Populations were small and life expectancy very low. It is easy to imagine that such coveted treasure defined nobility or important people in the village.

Some of us are old enough to remember who amongst our friends had the first telephone, the first television, the first DVD and so on. Intentional or not, owning these things were statements. Those people were the Joneses. I bet you can remember the names of those trailblazers. Conscious or not, when we see the benefits of this new technology we want to be in on it. If we didn't we'd all be living like the Amish.

Consumption and advertising go hand in hand. Everywhere we look some advertiser is trying to get our attention in order to part us from our hard-earned money. They try so hard on television that they blast the sound up louder than the programme they interrupted. Why should my viewing be interrupted every ten minutes by someone trying to sell me something I would rather not know about? I get very offended. I didn't invite them into my home, even if the mute button is activated. However, thankfully with so many alternatives it is little wonder people don't watch television any more.

Notice how people in ads shout at us. It is URGENT that we rush down to the mall to buy that bamboo pillow while it's half price. Hmm, we wonder if we want one. It is a good opportunity to try one. Especially while the price is so good. It's definitely worth trying at half price. If we don't like it we can give it away. Hello! We didn't know we wanted a bamboo pillow. Now we can't get the thing out of our heads. We spend the next morning driving to the mall – or jumping online since such a lot of us shop that way now. Once at the mall, or on the website, our senses are hopelessly bombarded with a myriad of other advertising. It's really difficult to concentrate on what we went in for. Next thing we know we've bought two bamboo pillows because the bed would look silly with just the one, and after all, we've only spent the equivalent of one bamboo pillow at the regular non-discounted price. Not only that, we've been enticed by the forty percent off kitchen appliance sale, the fifty percent off bathroom towel sale and the seventy five percent off cushion sale. Of course, all that shopping takes it out of us so we need to visit the food court. Then there is the wear and tear on our vehicle, the petrol consumed and our bank balance is now severely depleted. Now we have to work a total of three and a half days next week just to put ourselves in the same position financially as we were before we saw that stupid ad for the bamboo pillow.

Television ads are the prime reason I do not watch television. I don't even watch it for the news. The news is sensationalist. The newsreaders employed fit the media's preferred demographic. That is, young, slim, pretty and usually blonde. The bimbo clone delivers the narrative in sound bites between the more important advertising. The news is delivered in an excited and amplified tone. These days if we want in-depth coverage on a news item we need to search for it ourselves and thank goodness there are plenty of online platforms to enable that.

Happily there are other options for viewing programmes without advertising including Netflix, TV on Demand, Neon, Lightbox and Sky. You can control the amount of unwanted intrusion into your life. Frequently it's by engaging the off button. Silence really is golden. Try it. Where do your thoughts wander to? People say they have the radio on for company but anything other than the state broadcaster is peppered with ads, shock jocks and the hottest entertainment news, as if that makes any difference to your life. What would happen in your world if you missed one day of junk radio? I guarantee you would relax. Nothing changes in the world just because you don't know about it but there would be a change in you – for the better.

You have the choice of listening to the radio or not. You have the choice of turning on the television or not. Every decision you make is the result of a process that's occurred in your brain. We make thousands of decisions every day: we drive a car, shop, interact with other people, work. Before we open our mouths to speak we've processed what to say and how to say it depending on who we talk to.

Let's take a look at the decision making process. First we identify a need, or more than likely a want. Depending on our lifestyle or financial circumstances we then will need to make some choices about how that need can be fulfilled.

We collate information. Firstly we need to think where we can source the pertinent information then process it. Sometimes we end up with too much information which can easily sweep us off the track of the main objective. The information gathering stage involves a lot of work. Next we will identify alternatives and there could be many. Weighing the alternatives is the next step. In our heads we will imagine adopting each of the alternatives right through to the final outcome. This stage identifies the pros and cons of each alternative and identifies the risks associated with each. As we work through the alternatives and the risks associated with each, a priority will emerge. Now we can choose the alternative that will work best in achieving the desired outcome. At last, a decision has been made.

Time to take action. It could be as simple as placing the item into your shopping trolley, or it may be that we finance it somehow.

One last step. Review the decision and its consequences. Does our decision satisfy the objective of step one? Should we have sought more information or would one of the alternatives be better? You can see where shoppers in a supermarket review their decision at the checkout. Often there is an item that didn't fit all the criteria so was left on the checkout counter instead of making it all the way through into the shoppers bags.

We can suffer from decision fatigue without even knowing it. This has the paralysing effect of not even making a decision. Advertisers make it easy for us. Some advertisements for food show heart ticks or traffic lights so we don't need to read the nutritional panels. To our peril! Soap companies package their palm-oil soap products in fuzzy wuzzy eco-friendly packaging to prey on our laziness or decision fatigue.

Let's face it, after a day at work a trip to the supermarket is very unappealing. All we want is to get home and relax. At this stage of the day the quality of our decision making deteriorates. We have a reduced ability to make trade-offs. If every little decision had to go through the decision process outlined above we would be exhausted. So much easier to toss an impulse buy into the trolley, lured by whatever it takes to flick your switch. It could be ease of cooking, eco-friendly claims or price.

Alternatively it is possible to walk out with nothing. It's all just too hard. This used to happen to me when I went into cafés before I was vegan. I would stand in front of those rows of paninis, cakes and scones, completely overwhelmed and walk out the door with nothing. That was good for the waistline but I thought there was something wrong with me. Now I don't go into cafés because I know there won't be anything vegan for me to eat. Problem solved.

The interesting thing about making decisions is that it takes effort which consumes blood glucose, but this doesn't translate to physical fatigue. Therefore you don't realise that you are making poor quality decisions. If you think this really does not happen to you consider another scenario. Your wardrobe. How many times do you open the door, scan everything and exclaim, "I don't have anything to wear." Quite silly isn't it? What you mean is, "I have so many clothes I can't decide what to wear."

Here is an example of decision fatigue that tends to happen to me. I see somewhere I would like to go for an overseas holiday. It is not a package. That means I have to do some research, make some decisions. For a few weeks all my time is swallowed up researching the must see sights, transport, dollar exchange, accommodation and whether I am likely to maintain a good healthy vegan lifestyle. Suddenly it all seems just too hard and I am delighted not to be going anywhere. Should have just bought a ticket and gone while the impulse was strong. It is even worse when I tell someone that I am thinking of going somewhere. Suddenly I am bombarded with suggestions for what they consider would be a great holiday. The consequence of my decision fatigue is that I have hardly managed many overseas holidays at all.

Can I share another example of decision fatigue? I am sure you will recognise this. Your household is in the market for a new internet plan. You leave it to the expert in the house for this one. You know who I mean. The research that goes into this is relentless. He contacts every internet provider in the English speaking world for the best deal and compares our gigabyte usage with the International Space Station. At the end of every day this information is relayed to me for my interest. I should be interested in this, after all, I will be using data supplied by the internet service provider. Strangely, the expert's words disappear into the ether and his lips move without a sound. After weeks of polite head nodding I finally crack. I don't care. He chooses a company. Hooray. He has made a decision. But then he can't let it go. Researching internet plans has become a habit and he can't stop. Then horror of horrors, there is a better deal.

Minimalism provides freedom from choice without compromising freedom. The lifestyle banishes painful decision making and promotes liberty.

This chapter has been about the freedom to choose products. It is easy to buy products. Not so easy to get rid of them. To live in a de-cluttered house we need to stop buying. We can:

- Pay for non-essential items with cash (we don't like doing this and will think twice about it)

- Mute or switch off television and radio adverts

- Only buy quality items which will make you more inclined to treasure the item

- Switch the television and radio off for one day per week, or even for the whole week – when your attention isn't on these you start to notice the room you are in, the stuff that's in them. You will relax.

3

NECESSITY

"Contentment is not so much from great wealth as from few wants."
Epictetus, Greek Stoic philosopher,

55-135AD

Any worthy discussion on minimalism should include the concepts of needs and wants. I can assume that you wanted to buy this book. You had the money to purchase it, just as you had the money to purchase all the items that are now crowding your life.

There are many reasons we spend money. We have to spend money on food. This is a need. There is no getting away from it. If we don't want to starve to death we need to buy food. Other things, like this book, for example, we spend money on to gain some benefit. In this case the benefit is the knowledge gained from reading the book, whether you apply that knowledge or not. This is a want. You want the benefit of the book's contents but you don't need it. The benefit of spending the money on the book is weighed against not spending the money on the book. In other words, if the money was allocated to something else, how would you feel about missing out on the benefits of reading the book?

A purchase should be measured against what you can afford. It is all very well to purchase something when it has seventy percent off the price, but only on these provisos: you wanted the item in the first place, and you can afford it. You should think about how many hours you need to work in order to buy it. This has the immediate effect of illuminating how tied to consumerism we are. For example, take a large ticket item such as a fridge. It may be unaffordable to pay cash for a new fridge. There is an option, however, to pay a smaller amount weekly until it is paid off. Retailers who finance customers into purchases charge a high rate of interest so the customer ends up paying a lot more than the ticket price for the new fridge. The customer meanwhile, must keep her job for the next two years, or however long it is she took out the finance for, for fear of defaulting on the fridge payment and having it repossessed. Now she should take out a home contents insurance policy since if she couldn't afford the fridge in the first place, she can't afford for something to happen to it, for instance fall into disrepair due to flood, fire or earthquake, then she can't afford another one. She would be left in the unenviable position of paying off her loan for something she no longer owns. If you think this is rare, I'll let you into a little secret. It happens all the time with cars. The more we own the more we are beholden to our possessions.

Sometimes we spend money to make ourselves feel good. Shopping is a national sport in some countries. Annual and quarterly retail figures are tracked to gauge the health of our economy. Successive increases are seen as a good thing; an expanding economy, jobs for all. Successive decreases indicate a general gloominess that the economy will continue to soften, loss in jobs. Often the business cycle is tied to the political cycle. Note though, the word cycle. The economy swings and roundabouts. It always resets. The question is, how long does the good feeling last?

Sometimes it doesn't last very long. There is a very good reason that credit contracts have a cooling off period. This is the statutory seven days that a consumer has to get out of the contract they signed. Buyer's remorse is a recognised phenomenon. There can be many reasons for signing up for an item but in the cold light of day or after sleeping on it, the consumer realises they made a mistake. They can revoke the contract and reclaim any deposit paid. So, they felt good at the time they signed up for the item, then felt remorse, probably sick.

Some consumers feel good buying lots of small things from mail order companies. There is a thrill of a personally addressed envelope in the mailbox. Upon opening it an array of amazing gadgets is displayed in glossy colour. Everything is so appealing and affordable. And best of all it will be delivered to the mailbox. The thrill of a parcel in the post. We all know what that feels like. Mail order companies prey on older people who may not see other people every day. They understand the psychological needs of the elderly and they keep their customers engaged by personally addressing envelopes, engaging them in surveys and tricking them into believing they have won something.

Commonly we spend money on other people or causes to make us feel good. We want to make a difference so we donate money to charities. We want to believe that we are benevolent and kind.

There are people who live a hand to mouth existence and who probably live a minimalist lifestyle. But they don't choose their lifestyle in the same way that I do. They might refer to their circumstances as poor, or living in poverty. They don't choose to have their electricity cut off, or not to pay the school fees. The scant resources available to them have been allocated according to their priorities at the time, probably to pay for food or rent. Those are needs.

They want to pay the electricity bill but the fact is they can survive without it. They want to pay the school fees but no one is going to die if they aren't paid. Of course there is pressure to pay both of these but in the grand scheme of things, they are wants. Paying for a roof over their head and providing food for the family are priorities. These are needs.

The concept of wants versus needs is central to economic theory. Choices made by a collection of individuals is referred to as "the market" and it is the market that economists refer to when describing purchasing behaviour. Economics describes the consequences of the financial choices that we make, or what we do with our money based on a series of given facts. Therefore, economics is a social science rather than a pure science. It is also as backward looking as it is forward. Listen to any economist and she will forecast a downward housing market correction when the housing market gets over-heated, and an upward share market correction when indicators show the market has plummeted far enough.

As we have seen in the example above a need can be thought of as essential to life, with death being the alternative. A want can be thought of as those goods and services we would like to have but may or may not obtain. They are desires that cause business activities to produce such products and services that are demanded by us. Wants are unlimited of course, whilst the means to satisfy them are very limited.

When I was at university last century Bill Gates was worth a mere $US19 million. The reason I recall this figure was because my economics lecturer was trying to reinforce how relative the concept of want is. For instance, if Mr Gates wished to purchase a private island in the South Pacific which had an asking price of $US20 million he could not afford it. Under those circumstances you could say that he had only $US19 million – the emphasis being on only – and therefore could not afford to purchase what he wanted. With those funds available he would have to obtain finance for the balance of the price. Everyone it seems has wants that cannot be satisfied.

The most famous description of needs is an analysis by Abraham Maslow. In 1943 he produced a beautiful diagram commonly referred to today as Maslow's Hierarchy of Needs. Shown below, it is divided into two sections: the lower four levels are the deficiency needs. The theory is that one must rise through these levels before obtaining the freedom of the growth need which occupies the uppermost level.

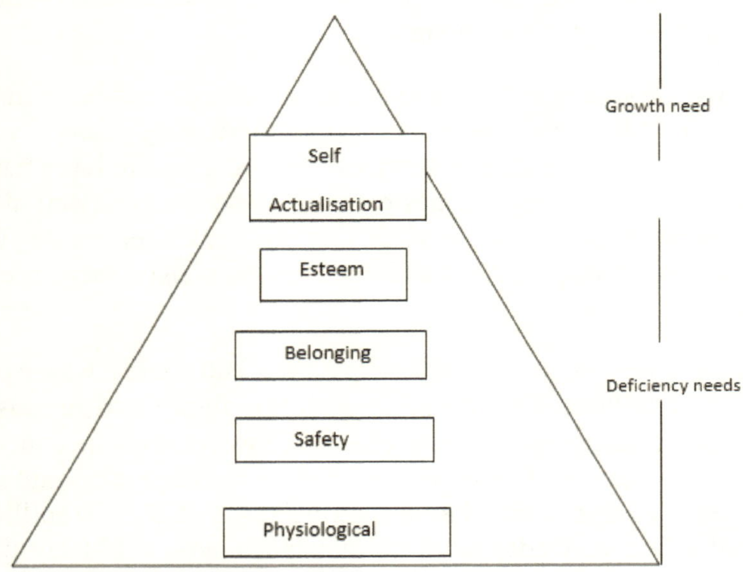

The diagram shows the five levels of needs that Maslow proposed in his Theory of Human Motivation. The idea is that we must move through all the levels in sequence to ultimately achieve self-actualisation.

The first and lowest level is the most basic that requires little explanation: Physiological. It refers to our physical needs. What do we need to survive? What can't we do without, that without it we could put our lives in such danger that we could die? It is three things that haven't changed since Homo Sapiens walked on two legs: food, water and shelter. These are needs that we seek to meet for ourselves and then later, for our mate and offspring.

Without water we can only survive three days and without food but with water twenty one days. We therefore need food and water to survive. Without shelter we would be subject not only to the vagaries of the weather, winter storms and blizzards, snowdrifts and heat waves, but also of the dangers that come with living on the streets, crime, disease and sickness.

To these three necessities we should add health and sleep for only with our own good health can we begin to care for others. Maslow said that we are motivated by necessity to fulfil our physiological needs. It is not an option to deny any of the needs, for then it would be impossible to progress to the next level.

Why does he choose safety as the next level and what does he mean by it? Remember we are moving up through a hierarchy of needs. Shelter was fulfilled in the first level so safety is physically assured by lease or by ownership of a house or apartment. This has come about presumably by one's ability to pay for such. In other words one has secured employment and is able to bring home a regular income. With this comes removal from danger. You are in a position to consider making a family, where they will be off the street and safe. The priority now moves to the health and well-being of the family. You look to be able to provide healthcare for them and to provide clothes. Nearly eighty years on from Maslow's theory, we take safety to also mean to be able to provide education for our children.

Maslow said the longer we are without a need the motivation to fulfil it becomes stronger. Once fulfilled our actions become habitualised into fulfilling the next need. Thus, the family lives in a house, and members are clothed and fed. The family can sleep at night safe in the knowledge that they won't be torn from their beds and thrown onto the street, and that there will be food on the table tomorrow. The provider is ready to progress to the next level.

This is being part of a group. There are many groups which sustain our needs. The first is family through which we find intimacy, affection and belonging. Through this we learn the social skills that serve us when we are ready to interact beyond the immediate family; there is school, work, maybe a sports team and leisure pursuits. With these there is acceptance within the group. It is not enough for humans to belong only to a family group. As part of the primate family we thrive on being part of a larger social group and we all want to be accepted by other members of that group.

The last level in Maslow's growth needs is esteem. By that he means to have esteem for oneself and the respect of others. Here

Maslow divides esteem into lower and upper; the lower being a desire to have the respect of others. A person craves status, recognition, fame and prestige. Alternately, the higher esteem relates to self respect. A person may desire strength, mastery and self confidence. Respect for and by others is reward for having moved through all the levels. You are the person people ask for favours. Your opinion is valued. You are dependable, trustworthy, reliable. You have proven that you can look after yourself and others. You have valuable life experience.

At the top of Maslow's Hierarchy of Needs he has placed self-actualisation. This is reached only after all the lower levels have been achieved. Only now are you able to achieve your full individual potential. Time can now be spent on creativity and problem solving. One can look outside one's own physical and emotional needs and devote time to others in the social group. Unless one's needs are met up through the levels, one would be unable to spend time unselfishly in the service of others.

Maslow developed the hierarchy of needs amidst World War II and long before the emergence of consumerism. It was probably Maslow's experience that people never wasted food and patched clothes rather than threw them away, even nylon stockings. For most of history people have lived frugally and it is only in wealthy industrialised nations that people don't live this way. But this is changing. Consumerism is being challenged by movements such as minimalism and environmentalism.

Wants

Where are you in Maslow's continuum? At least half way up the pyramid and beyond is my guess. If you've accumulated enough surplus stuff you must feel secure enough to divert funds to goods other than food and shelter. In fact you've felt so confident that you've engaged in a totally new phenomenon – comfort buying. Buying stuff made you feel good. It looked good in the shop. It doesn't look so good now that you've got it home. You thought you wanted it. You didn't know you wanted it until you saw it in the shop, beautifully displayed along with ten others exactly the same.

Sadly, I hear you. This is what you can say as you stand in the shop admiring that beautiful dust collector."It will never look as good at home as it does in this shop." That's true! What makes it look so fabulous in the shop is that there's ten of them, the light is aimed right on it, the background paint is just the right colour and the beautiful displays all around it complement it like nothing could at home. Leave it in the shop. Leave it there and know that you could never do it justice at home. It goes from being a want to a burden. Pick it up, admire it, then with great aplomb, return it to the display shelf knowing it will never ever look so good at your house.

Not only that. It will upset the balance within your home that you have taken great pains to achieve. If you introduce something new it will demand space to show it off effectively. Another item will have to either move or be eliminated to restore harmony.

The Anti-minimalism Argument

There seems to be a murmur of anti-minimalism at the moment. Some people are disparaging of our attempts to live a simpler, more meaningful life by pointing out that minimalism is a middle class western phenomenon; that minimalism is for rich people.

That some countries are richer than others is undeniable. Each year a list of the richest countries in the world is published by *Fortune Magazine*. The criteria to determine wealth is based on International Monetary Fund data with GDP (gross domestic product) per capita based on purchasing power parity. The formula for GDP is the sum of all spending on goods and services in a nations' economy in a year:

GDP = C + I + G + (Exports-Imports)

      Spending   investments   government   net exports

         by   by

      consumers   business

In 2017 the top ten richest countries according to Fortune Magazine were:

1. Qatar

2. Luxembourg

3. Singapore

4. Brunei

5. Ireland

6. Norway

7. Kuwait

8. United Arab Emirates

9. Switzerland

10. Hong Kong

There are obvious factors behind the wealth of these countries; oil and finance. According to Fortune Magazine New Zealand comes in at number 35, behind Puerto Rico and ahead of Spain. However, according to the World Bank, using different assumptions New Zealand ranked 28th, and according to the International Monetary Fund New Zealand ranked 31st.

Interestingly, hardly any of the above countries make the top ten happiest in the world. Each year the United Nations Sustainable Development Solutions Network publishes the World Happiness Report. It is based on a survey of six key variables that support well-being. These are income, healthy life expectancy, social support, freedom, trust and generosity. In 2017 Finland had the happiest inhabitants, followed in order by Norway, Denmark, Iceland, Switzerland, the Netherlands, Canada, New Zealand, Sweden and Australia. It is striking that the only countries to make both lists are Norway and Switzerland. Perhaps it is the beauty of landscape, who knows. But one thing is clear: money does not equate to happiness.

It's also true that certain sectors of society would be drawn to minimalism. Notice the selected quotes under the chapter headings. Many of those quoted were born into privilege and gave up the distraction of things in favour of a more meaningful life. They saw around them people with comparatively little. They recognised that the ownership of stuff is a burden that brings responsibilities and not necessarily happiness or meaning to a life.

One must be responsible for one's items, ensure they are stored correctly away from potential damage. If it is valuable it should be insured against theft or breakage separately from the general household insurance. Insurance therefore, is a co-requisite of ownership and it is something that must be paid for as a privilege of ownership. The item needs to be kept in good condition as proof that it is a reverential piece

In all countries, wealthy or poor, there will always be sections of society that occupy every level of Maslow's Hierarchy of Needs. It is a natural progression of finding one's feet in the world. There are reasons that some people find themselves unable to transcend out of the bottom level. For whatever reason, poor life choices, or personal tragedy, some people never get beyond providing for their own physiological needs, and for some even shelter is something unachievable.

The fact that this occurs in western countries might be a source of shame for some anti-minimalists, but to say that minimalism is only for the rich is wrong. There are many ways that stuff is accumulated. It is often inherited. Grandma's possessions are novel, well made and hold special value for the recipient. They transport the holder to another time and place and they can be difficult to part with, particularly if the feelings evoked are warm and fuzzy. Thus, even people situated in Maslow's lowest rungs have the ability to accumulate stuff.

Creative people hoard stuff to use in the creation of yet more stuff. It is very hard for creative people to downsize their collection of useful stuff because although it isn't in use right now, they can visualise its use in the future. According to Maslow, expressing creativity can only be possible when physiological needs are met. Therefore this can be found in the belonging level, where participants have the wherewithal to join groups outside the home.

The recognition of the difference between needs and wants is a powerful tool. Wants have the ability to propel us forward in the world. They don't have to relate to a physical article. The want to succeed in a career or activity, in education or any endeavour we choose is fuelled by the want to achieve something worthwhile that will make us feel good about ourselves. To that end there will be steps along the way that need to be completed. This is expressed in Maslow's self-actualisation category at the pinnacle of the pyramid. Self-actualisation simply means the realisation or fulfilments of one's talents and potentialities. It is expressed as the drive or a need within us.

As I said, economics is the study of predicting what a bunch of consumers is likely to do given a set of choices. It looks backwards to see what has happened in the past. Maslow's Hierarchy is simply a reflection of behaviour. You will be able to think of it when next faced with a purchasing dilemma. Picture it and mull over needs and wants.

So how can we relate the above discussion to ourselves on a day to day level? Of course to follow the minimalist ethos the idea is not to purchase a whole lot of stuff we don't need. Ownership of stuff is a burden. Here are some thoughts around reducing the compulsion to purchase:

- Calculate how many hours of work it would take to pay for the item you want

- Purchase with cash if possible

- Praise how nice the item looks in the shop and leave it at that. It won't look that good at your house

- Consider whether the proposed purchase needs separate insurance and whether you can afford the associated expense

4

CONSUMERISM

"The philosophy of materialism offers no raisin d'etre for human existence."Pope Benedict XVI, (1927-)

There are many reasons to become minimalist and you might be struck by just one. But once you begin the journey a light goes on inside your head and you begin to implement many different aspects. You don't know what options are available to you unless they are already part of your experience. If you grow up in a household where the television and radio are always on you are denied the sensory pleasure of silence. Silence has a calming influence over us. It is golden and it can also be loud. You hear your thoughts and there is no distraction in pursuing them.

There is something else that happens when the television and radio are switched off. The house is not filled with advertising propaganda. Notice this. It is a powerful realisation. It is a small but mighty first step into removing yourself from the consumer machine. The what? What do I mean by consumer machine?

I have already talked about consumerism and how I see western culture as a consumerist culture but what is it actually? One definition is that it is a social or economic order and ideology that encourages the acquisition of goods and services in ever increasing amounts. There are all sorts of finance schemes and lending institutions to assist you in your never ending quest of acquisition. Pretty soon you are trapped in the work spend cycle. The minute you borrow money to purchase something you are locked into work. You have to work, sometimes at a job you hate, just to satisfy, not only your landlord, but your lender. It makes you scared to leave the certainty the job brings, which leads to stress and dissatisfaction. Now all you want to do is to pay off that fridge so you can go back to feeling how you felt before the loan weighed you down.

Note that the definition of consumerism refers to a social order. We are not alone. Consumerism is the new order, the new way of things. Evidence of it is everywhere around us. It's in advertising and the latest fashions. Everywhere we look someone is trying to get us to buy something. Bill boards are massive, even taking up the whole sides of buildings in some overseas cities. Television and radio commercials are loud and shout at us with urgency. Try getting rid of the flashing advertisements on news websites, or any website for that matter. They demand to know why you don't want to see that ad and others just pop up in their place. They are designed to make us feel inferior if we don't rush out and purchase their wares. Yes, marketing has its place and some of the things we enjoy wouldn't exist without the marketing dollar. But that is not the focus of this chapter. We are concerned with how we can reduce our spending on stuff we don't need.

There is a flip side: anti-consumerism. It is a socio-political ideology opposed to the continual buying and consuming of material possessions particularly where environmental practices, animal rights, social justice and ethics are compromised. Whenever you make a purchase you become a consumer. As we have plenty of choice in absolutely everything available for purchase, we barely register the effort that went into producing a product. We don't think beyond the immediate use the product has. We don't mentally trace the supply chain all the way back to the raw material, via the mining or growing of the base material, the process that added value to it to turn it into something we want or the myriad of ticket clippers getting it to market. Some goods require vast amounts of advertising to you the consumer to try to persuade you that you need them. In fact without that advertising you didn't even know it existed let alone wanted it.

It's nothing new. In newspapers one hundred years ago, peppered between the grim news of World War I, were screeds of advertisements for conditions and complaints a person never knew existed. Here is an example from the *Auckland Star* 13 February 1918.This page was in the women's section and took up four equivalent columns or half a page.

Baxter's Lung Preserver – children's colds would be banished.

Biff – this was for tender, tired, sore, swollen or perspiring feet, and corns and chilblains. It relieved without delay.

Mother Seigel's Syrup – this could be taken for indigestion, bilious attacks, a heavily coated tongue, a nauseous taste in the mouth, disagreeable eructations, retching, vomiting or an undermined system.

Oatine Face Cream – will bring beauty to the plainest face and a velvety softness to the toughest hands.

Beachams' Pills – to tone up the stomach when it is deranged or jaded with overwork, correct the action of the liver when it is sluggish and they effectively clean the bowels when disordered by constipation.

John Craven Burleigh's True Hair Grower – for loss of hair, dandruff, thin straggling weak hair, split hairs, over-greasiness of the scalp and over-dryness or itching of the scalp, loss of colour and lustre.

The poor housewife reading that could be excused for thinking there should be something wrong with her. Doesn't it make you check your tongue in the mirror?

The power of advertising is undisputed. Companies pay big money to develop brands, then more big money to secure prime advertising, naming rights, or the purchase of sports teams. In any university you will find marketing degrees and experts on the psychology of marketing – or to read between the lines – how to part the consumer with their hard earned cash to buy a product they didn't want in the first place.

It's in these disciplines where you'll encounter terms like systematic obsolescence, programmed obsolescence, perceived obsolescence, functional obsolescence and of course planned obsolescence.

Systematic obsolescence is where there is an upgrade to a system which will not be compatible with a component that you already have. Telecommunications and software industries are classic examples here. Technology changes so quickly we are forced to upgrade even when we don't want to. It is tough to be a consumer here. You're either in or out. There are no other options.

Certain products are designed to be replaced after a specified time or use, for example, ink cartridges. This is an example of programmed obsolescence. Brilliant business technique for the seller, terrible for the production of waste. There is a requirement to make ever more replacement products. There is more mining of natural resources and more pollution. The shorter the replacement cycle, the greater the environmental footprint. Again, it is tough to be a consumer when the manufacturer puts themselves first.

Obsolescence of function is something devised when a product is being planned. Each component of a product, for example, a kitchen appliance, phone, or camera will have a limited life. It is known from the outset when a component will wear out. The manufacturer ensures that it is not in the consumer's interest to repair the item, thus a replacement can be sold. Gone are the days when a toaster, camera or watch was taken to a specialist repairer.

The fashion industry relies on perceived obsolescence. If the consumer perceives something as out of date they won't buy it. Jeans are a classic example of a product that is continually redesigned to appeal to new generations of wearers. Blue jeans have been around since the cowboy but the only thing that has stayed the same is they are made of denim and have two legs. Over the centuries every adaptation has been made to the style, the cut, the ornamentation and the functionality to broaden their appeal to men, women, children and other.

Packaging and the method of delivery of goods are continually updated by marketers. How many times have you stood in the cleaning aisle of the supermarket bewildered at the endless and dazzling display of specialist cleaners that all shout that they are the best? There is no denying the packaging is attractive. More than that, it's beguiling. The colours dazzle, the cans stand beautifully upright like tin soldiers, all facing the front, the better to attract attention of the wary shopper who has already spent this week's budget on fruit and vegetables.

But wait, there is something new and innovative. The newest improvement in dispensing the same old cleaning product: a minor development to the trigger so the liquid doesn't drip. What an advance! What a must have! Certainly makes all the other products seem obsolete.

Making Sense of Too Many Products

Let's take a common old garden variety of household cleaner. When you read the back panel are you any wiser? How many of us have a chemistry degree? I found the ingredients for Ajax Spray 'n Wipe which is freely available on the internet. See if you recognise any.

Water	for consistency
Lactic acid	natural anti-bacterial agent
Sodium dodecyl benzene sulphonate	a cleaning agent – anionic surfactant, synthetic detergent
Dipropylene glycol butyl ether	a cleaning solvent – used in surface coatings, leather, pesticides, electrical, industrial cleaners, resins and printing inks
Alcohols, C10-12, ethoxylated	cleaning agents – emulsifier/surfactant used in laundry detergents, surface cleaners, cosmetics, textiles, paint
Ethanol	cleaning solvent – chemical name for alcohol, anti-bacterial, effective against most bacteria, fungi and many viruses

Sodium laureth sulphate (palm oil)	cleaning agent
Fragrance	for nice scent
Sodium hydroxide (lye or caustic soda)	pH adjuster – highly caustic substance used to neutralise acids and make sodium salts. At room temperature it absorbs moisture from the air. pH is a scale of acidity from 0-14. It tells how acidic or alkaline a solution is. Neutral is 7, acidic is less than 7, alkaline is more than 7. (Rainwater is 5.6)

Chemical data explanations from:

https://wwwpubchem.org – open chemistry database

https://www.hazmap.n/m.nih.govt – US National Library of Medicine

Water I recognise. I have plenty of that. Lactic acid I recognise, as it is a build up of acid in muscles. I have exercised and I know this. As to the rest, there is a nasty in there: palm oil. Palm plantations have such a destructive ecological footprint that I will cover that in the Envrionmental chapter. I do not use any product that has palm oil in it.

I have managed to whittle down my cleaning cupboard to the following:

Windows:	One tablespoon of white vinegar in water. The acidity of vinegar allows it to dissolve minerals from glass and other surfaces. It is highly alkaline and is a very good grease cutter.
Sanitiser:	Undiluted white vinegar (natural anti-bacterial agent)

Floors, walls, toilet:	One teaspoon washing soda dissolved in two cups hot water. Add a squirt of liquid soap. Washing soda is sodium carbonate or soda ash. It has the chemical formula Na2Co3. It is available from bulk food shops.
Hard to shift marks:	Baking soda mixed with as much liquid soap as it takes to make a soft scouring lotion.

Making your own household cleaners is a good first step in thumbing your nose at rampant consumerism. It's quick to make a batch of washing soda cleaner or liquid scourer and it's much cheaper. Of course, it's also a great feeling to know that you are not introducing chemicals into your house.

Shampoo

Shampoo is a classic case of being duped into buying something we don't need. I have been shampoo free for eleven years. The first thing I noticed was that my hair became lighter in colour from dark strawberry blonde to light strawberry blonde. After years of not particularly liking the shampoo colour I delighted in the new look, which should be of no surprise when I figured out what was going on. I was the victim of the shampoo cycle. I now had my real natural colour back. And people thought I'd dyed my hair blonde!

Here's a very quick rundown on shampoo. They contain harsh, drying sulphates which are foaming agents. Hair follicles contain natural oil called sebum. Shampoo strips away this oil which then activates the sebum into producing more oil to replace that which was lost. And what does oil do, apart from making your hair oily? It makes it dark.

This is what I found makes up shampoo:

- Ammonium chloride – white salt highly soluble in water, mildly acidic, fertiliser

- Ammonium lauryl sulphate – foaming agent, surfactant (helps water mix with oil). Sulphates are drying because they strip oil from the hair. Can be made from coconut but also in the laboratory.

- Glycol – any class of organic compounds that belong to the alcohol family. Found in cosmetics as a solvent, preservative and a moisture-retaining agent. It is used to attract water to the hair.

- Sodium lauryl sulphate (Palm oil) – SLS – an irritant surfactant used to promote foaming action.

- Sodium laureth sulphate (Palm oil) – SLES – a surfactant gentler than SLS derived from palm oil fruit. Irritant on skin and eyes. Used to increase foaming action.

- Sodium lauroamphoacetate – surfactant, mild cleaning agent

- Polysorbate 20 (PEG (20)) - used as an emulsifier (components that hold products together by preventing oil and water from separating. Twenty parts ethylene oxide.

- Polysorbate 80 (PEG (80))

- Polysorbate 150 (PEG (150))

- Citric acid – weak organic acid occurring naturally in fruit. Active ingredient in chemical peels.

- Quaternium-15 – an ammonium salt used as a surfactant and preservative in cosmetic and industrial substances. Anti-microbial agent by virtue of being a formaldehyde releaser. Source of skin irritant and allergic reactions.

- Polyquaternium-10 – water soluble, white granulated powder. Anti-static and moisturising properties. Film former supplying sheen and coating to hair strands by being easily absorbed by proteins.

- Di-PPG-2 myreth-10 – surfactant, skin conditioning emollient having the quality of softening the skin.

- Meth glisothiazolinone – preservative, sanitiser.

That's a lot of surfactants. They are compounds used in cleaning products for their ability to lower the surface tension of water molecules. This makes the molecules slippery and they are less likely to stick to each other and more likely to interact with oil and grease.

Staggering isn't it? There are more ingredients in shampoo to clean your hair than there are to clean your entire house.

Here is the recipe for my hair cleaner: baking soda, water. Yes, you read that correctly. The alternative to shampoo is simply baking soda. I keep some in a jar in the shower and use about a teaspoon scooped into my hand before rubbing it through my hair. Baking soda removes excess oil. Then to condition I pour a fifty fifty mix of apple cider vinegar and water into my cupped hand then rinse my hair with that. I usually use two handfuls. The apple cider vinegar restores the pH balance.

My hair is very fine, the flyaway variety so I always use a leave in conditioner such as coconut oil. In fact once a week I deep condition my hair with coconut oil, leaving quite a lot in my hair for hours. After it is washed out my hair is super soft. Before you rush into trying this method you should do your own research. There is a lot of information available. Just be aware of who is putting out the information and what their agenda is. As with everything, there are pros and cons.

I wouldn't consider buying a bottle of shampoo now and you know what? No one has ever come up to me and said my hair needs a wash.

Not having to make agonising decisions over which floor cleaner or shampoo to buy is pure delight. I simply glide past these aisles and feel sorry for the people trapped in them.

Marketing Psychology of Supermarket Shopping

You probably have a set routine to carry out the task of grocery shopping. More than likely you go on the same day at the same time every week, whether or not you need to. Think back to when this routine began. Was it because your pay hit your bank account that day? The toddlers were at pre-school?

Supermarkets recognise this and they go to great lengths to control you. From layout to product placement, music to baking smells. Everything is designed to distract you from your list. That means buying stuff that isn't on your list. Nothing that happens inside a supermarket is left to chance. Supermarkets employ psychologists and behaviourists to devise ways to get us to spend more money.

Let's start with the exterior of the building. Warm colours draw us in. We want to be inside a nice safe environment. Once inside however, the warm colours are nowhere to be seen. This is because cool colours invite us to contemplate and the longer we contemplate the longer we are inside the store which means there is more chance of purchasing stuff we don't need.

Now that they've got us in there they manipulate our sense of quantity. When did shopping trolleys get so big? They are designed to cart the big stuff but also to cart more of the small stuff. A small amount of groceries looks ridiculous at the bottom of the trolley. It might be everything you need but it doesn't look it because you can still see the bottom of the trolley. The trend now has gone away from the giant trolleys that some of us can't reach the bottom of to friendlier, easier to manoeuvre small trolleys. In fact there are now multiple sizes of small trolleys. Presumably this is to trick us into thinking we have everything we need when we don't, then need to return to the supermarket before the week is out. The result is more spending on impulse buys. Why make use of a well proven ruse only once a week?

Right from the minute you drive that trolley into the shop you're trapped. There's even a little metal gate that opens as you push through. But try to push out and you can't. They're designed to trap you in.

But at this juncture you're happy to be there. A visual symphony greets you. The flower section welcomes you in with a delightful smell. This lifts your mood and when your spirits are high you spend more. Also, flowers are a high margin commodity so the supermarket wants the best chance to part you from your cash before you realise you've reached your spending limit.

The bakery is also designed to lure you in. The smells from the flower department and the bakery activate your salivary glands. Research shows that this helps you purchase goods impulsively. Clever huh!

The beautiful smells you've encountered in your first few minutes have put you in a good mood. The supermarket needs you to be in a good mood so you will spend more money.

Notice how fruit and vegetables are one of the first things you encounter. Again, this is by design, not chance. This is pleasant to look at and has the feel of a street market. It's all very nice and mood enhancing. Just for a minute imagine encountering the cleaning aisle in its place. Made you feel a bit flat didn't it. A bit hum drum, a bit yuck. Well the supermarket psychologists know this. They know that your purchasing decisions from that point on would be pragmatic, automatic and you'd be out of that store like a rocket. They don't want that. That's why it's fruit and vegetables.

You'll notice essentials like bread on the back wall. We have to traipse through the whole store to get to it and you know what that means: more distraction, more opportunity to purchase something you otherwise wouldn't have.

The aisles are another trap. They are designed to be walked like an airport check in. No deviations allowed. Herd us like cows is what the supermarket wants. And now that we're in those psychedelic tunnels it's a different game. It comes down to the minutiae of product placement on the shelves.

At eye level are the goods the supermarket wants you to buy. You have to look quite hard to find the cheap stuff. That is at the bottom with the bulk goods. You need to bend your knees to get that stuff. And the expensive stuff – that's at the top, being more exclusive type products. Then there is the question of how far along the aisle the goods are positioned. For example coffee is always half way down. You'll never find it on the ends. The supermarket wants you to walk past dozens of new products as you head for the coffee. Remember coffee is the world's second most consumed commodity.

Don't think that children are not in the supermarkets' targets. There is an eye level position just for them. This is where you'll find brightly coloured appealing sugary unhealthy snacks.

On certain days of the week there may be sample stations. I notice these on weekends when supposedly we have more time to shop. They slow you down. You engage with the vendor. A strong shopper has the ability to say no after having sampled the freebie. A sensible shopper wouldn't have stopped.

Do supermarkets appear to be getting bigger or is it that the shopping trolleys have shrunk? Retail space has a value per square metre and within the store its layout dictates that some areas are worth more than others. It may pay to maximize the space by cramming in more shelves in high population density locations. However, people are funny beasts. Some cultures don't cope with crowds as well as other cultures do. Thus the supermarkets tailor to this quirk. In New Zealand the aisles are wide and there is ample space to browse without being jostled by other shoppers. We simply wouldn't spend time in supermarkets if we couldn't have our personal space. We'd be in and out, never having deviated from the list.

Music. The classic mood enhancer. Supermarkets play different styles of music for the different demographics that are in their stores at a particular time. Psychologists have determined that classical music makes people purchase higher value products, that fast music makes us shop faster and slow music makes us shop slower. Remember the slower we shop, the more time we spend inside the store and the more opportunity to be exposed to new products and purchase goods impulsively.

Phew! You've nearly made it to the checkout. But you're not out yet. The checkout aisle, as short as it is, is the most profitable area.

There are magazines you might browse as you wait in the queue, cold drink machines, kitchen gadgets that you're supposed to toss into your trolley at the last minute and of course confectionary. You have plenty of time to gaze longingly at the beautiful display of shiny wrappers. This is your reward for having completed yet another weekly shop.

Lastly you swipe your rewards or club card. You may as well. You've not anything to lose, right? You have to grocery shop. Fact is, you've nothing to gain, not really. The supermarket tracks your spend and give you a few paltry cents off. But for them they've got your loyalty. They've got you for life.

Or maybe not. There are a few things you can do to regain control over your grocery shopping. You don't have to shop every single week. You can break the habit. I only shop when I've run out of cat food. I can get by for a few days more than a week if I have to. I can eat the house out, but when there's nothing in the cupboard or the freezer for my boys I just have to gird my loins and hit the supermarket. I don't have a routine.

You can buy your fruit and vegetables from specialist shops. I do so two to three times per week. This keeps a small business owner in business and my produce is always fresh. I never throw out rotting fruit and vegetables. They don't have time to go bad. It also engenders a relationship with the shop keeper who proudly stands by her produce. Having to compete with supermarkets ensures good customer service.

You don't have to be sucked into the cleaning aisle where people spend too much time deliberating over the impossible marketing claims. At the end of the day it's you who has to do the cleaning. The product isn't going to magically hop off the laundry shelf, pour itself into a bucket of hot water then throw itself onto the floor. You have to use elbow grease to clean anything. So you may as well stop kidding yourself. Make your own cleaning products. Say goodbye to the cleaning aisle, goodbye to outlandish marketing claims and hello to regaining some control over your own life.

I don't buy meat because I am vegan but if I did I would support the small business owner who stands by her product. Once you develop a rapport with these people they look after you. I dare you to try it.

Remember, in order to live a de-cluttered life we need to reduce the amount of stuff we purchase in the first place. Being aware of marketing techniques helps us understand how we are manipulated. Nothing about selling a product is left to chance from the packaging to its placement in the shop. The awareness arouses curiosity around the product itself. What is the story behind it? Can you find or make a replacement that is planet friendly? I discussed two products that are recent inventions: shampoo and household cleaners. I hope that when you see advertisement for these now you will recall this chapter on consumerism.

Here are some practical things to implement:

- Reduce your exposure to advertising inside your own home

- Vow not to buy certain "hyped" up products, for example specialised glass cleaner when hot water and vinegar will do the job, or shampoo when baking soda will do

- Read the backs of packages. If you don't understand what you are reading, don't buy it

- Use a list to grocery shop

- Find out if your supermarket does a low sensory hour for shoppers with special needs. If it does, great. It not, request it

5

SOCIAL CONSCIENCE

"There's nothing I can't live without. I learned this attitude when I was a child. When you practice contentment you can say to yourself, Oh yes, I already have everything that I really need." Dalai Lama, incumbent since 1940

"Our life is frittered away by details. Simplify. Simplify. I make myself rich by making my wants few." Henry Thoreau (Walden) Philosopher 1817-1862

You might be asking what social conscience has to do with living minimally. Social conscience is a sense of responsibility and concern for the problems and injustices of the broader institutions of society. That seems to be a lofty ideal for someone who wants to de-clutter their house but the actions we engage in can reflect the greatest benefit to ourselves at the expense of other individuals or a lesser benefit to ourselves with some benefits to others. For example when we buy cheap plastic goods from the $2.00 shop it reinforces the fact that we don't care about the production of that item because it has saved us money, since we didn't buy a quality, perhaps ethically produced equivalent. If we purchase goods with the makers of those goods in mind, chances are we will make more ethical choices and purchase less rubbish and more quality which we would be inclined to keep. The focus of this chapter is ethical purchasing. Every dollar we spend can be a vote for justice if we understand how those goods are produced.

Conspicuous consumption is a recent phenomenon. Consume comes from the Latin verb consumer, to waste or use up. The terms planned obsolescence and throwaway society would have left our Edwardian forebears scratching their heads. What do we mean by planned obsolescence? Why on earth would anyone plan for an object to become obsolete when many hours went into manufacturing it, from sourcing the materials, planning and pattern making to the construction and detail of finish. No matter what the product is, the stages in getting it into the hands of the consumer remains the same.

The motor car industry is expert at planned obsolescence; they've been doing it longer than anyone else. The giant carmakers, particularly of 1950s America, could afford to woo the consumer with minor changes to a car year on year. They tap into the buyer's psyche to sell purely on sex appeal what is essentially a metal box on wheels, able to transport humans from one place to another. And it works! We upgrade our cars for no good reason other than to feel good. The motor industry knows that. They aren't going to keep building 1940 model Buicks forever, even though going by the requirements of a motor vehicle, they could. So they persuade us that we need this year's model, for whatever reason, and our faithful motor car which hasn't yet died, is destined for the scrap yard.

I am not sure that many electric car owners have thought about this but all they need to replace is the battery after about ten years. The chassis and body will probably last sixty or seventy years. The battery issue at present isn't one of planned obsolescence. It's just where we are with technology. Hopefully EV owners are not sucked into the hype of new car marketing. If the car does what you want it to do and it's only the battery that is near the end of its life, why replace the entire car?

Similarly, the term throwaway society. Sounds mad doesn't it? I think the best thing to do to reinforce how lightly we value the manufactured product is to walk into a $2.00 shop. It is quite overwhelming. Your first thought is "how can anyone make this stuff for $2.00?" I know, it's crazy. Then you see something you think you might want. You have to think, do you really want it, or is it because it's so cheap you can simply have it. Never before in human history have we had the ability to purchase something just because it was cheap. And even if we aren't sure whether we want it or not, it's no great risk financially if we get it home and find it was rubbish, or we didn't like the colour, so we biff it out. Yep: throwaway society.

When did this happen? It hasn't always been like this. Let's wander back to the time when we were agriculturists living a subsistence lifestyle. We'd have been up at the crack of dawn, milked the cow, collected the eggs and got the fire going in the house before trudging outside to tend to the wheat or maize or rice. We would have donned the same clothes as yesterday and worked with ploughs, rakes and spades that our grandfathers used. When the day was over we'd light candles which had been re-melted and refashioned. Very little was available. Nothing was wasted. Nothing was taken for granted.

It was 1712 when the age of steam ushered in a bright new world. An astute chap noticed a pot of water boiling. The lid was being forcefully elevated by the bubbling hot water. He recognised this as energy being produced. Hmm, he thought to himself. If something as fundamental as steam can lift a pot lid what else can it do?

Thomas Newcomen ushered in a new age of industrialisation with his steam engine which was used to pump water from coal mines. Agricultural equipment, which had been around since man fashioned metal into ploughs and hoes, now became mechanised, although it was a little while yet before the new fad caught on. The race was on to invent machines to assist humans, to make our lives better. The first such machine to revolutionise production was the spinning Jenny in 1764. This was used in the production of textiles, principally English wool. The new contraption could spin more than one thread at a time and the days of homespun wool, tenderly worked of an evening in a small croft or cottage were numbered. Now, forevermore the great industrialist capitalists would own the means to that production.

Factories were located adjacent to rivers with a good flow on which a large waterwheel was installed. Connected to this was a series of arms and cogs that fed into the factory to drive the new miracle spinning textile machines.

The factories attracted rural workers; women, children and their male overseers. Conditions were poor and they worked long hours in dusty, poorly ventilated and poorly lit workshops for little pay. But why did they do that? Why did they trade an independent but subsistence lifestyle working on small farms for one of long hours in poor light, cramped and even dangerous conditions? The answer is to avoid famine. Crops weren't always guaranteed. Sometimes a small holding couldn't produce enough to feed the farmer and his family let alone produce a surplus for market. Also, farmers rarely owned their own land. They were serfs to the landowner who sold the crops. So it made sense for them to try working in the new factories. Money earned was theirs to allocate how they liked. New products flooded the market in response to the new workforce; mass produced clothes, baking in tins, sweets, mechanised horses. Suddenly people could choose the convenience of buying something readymade with their new money. So began the slippery slope of consumerism.

Work was noisy as the mechanical parts clacked together and it was dangerous. The factory owners wouldn't allow the machines to stop so blockages and tangles would be cleared by the smallest workers who could duck and dive amidst the moving parts – children.

Thirty years later came the introduction of the cotton gin and America joined the industrial revolution. It wasn't until 1846 that Elias Howe invented the foot pedal sewing machine. This was a defining moment in the production of garments. No longer was a woman able to stay home and make clothes for the textile producer. She could spend all day in a cold noisy factory sewing piecemeal. Then, in 1879 the means of production was thrown another bone. An electric light that lasted until the switch was turned off was invented. Workers could work until they dropped from exhaustion.

Imagine this Dickensian scene today. Instead of a cold grey English day, it's a hot Bangladeshi day, sweltering hot inside the factory as well as outside. Great mechanical fans are inset in the walls. Women, brightly garbed with heads covered, sit at sewing machines while young men stalk the factory floor, inspecting their work, keeping them working. This is the modern face of fast fashion.

And we don't treat those clothes reverently. The world is awash with garments made from cheap labour. There is nothing special about them. No special skill required since a worker only sews one piece. Nothing difficult about sewing sleeves into a shirt when it is all you do all day, every day. This makes labour cheap and unvalued.

The rag trade is synonymous with the unethical treatment of workers. However, as more of the world's population enjoys a discretionary income, the more important ethical purchasing becomes. The tide is slowly turning as consumers become aware of the plight of the workers who make their clothes.

People in western countries in particular are voting for better treatment of third world workers by purchasing clothes made ethically. In other words they are exercising their moral responsibility in their financial decisions.

Ethically produced clothing is not in the consumers' face. You don't see shops with accreditation logos on their windows or even on advertising inside the shop. It's not easy for consumers to find or be aware of ethically made clothes. They tend to be high end products. You have to put yourself out to find them. One highlight each year is during New Zealand Fashion Week. The topic is typically raised at that time. Other than that, you have to do your own investigations.

There are a plethora of fashion labels that can claim fair trade and are accredited so. Accreditation doesn't simply apply to the treatment of factory workers. Some accreditations encompass environmental standards, from the type of seed grown to produce the cotton, to the types of weed and pest control. Then there is the transport to the clothing factory, how all the workers are treated, and the treatment of the workers at the distribution warehouse. Finally the garments will travel by sea across the world. Many people handle the garments from the beginning of the supply chain to the garment hanging in a High Street shop. Where the garments are accredited as being ethical the purchaser can be confident that the extra money she pays goes to the farmer and the workers along the supply chain. It costs the supplier good money for its moral certifications and accreditations. We should expect to pay more for all the effort gone into producing ethical garments.

Here are some brands that you might not be familiar with that have socially conscious ethics: Ovna-Ovish, WE-AR, Mane Project, Grumpysuns, Outliv and Tonic & Cloth.

But what if it doesn't have an ethical accreditation? New Zealand is awash with cheap clothing imports and they aren't just a little bit cheaper, they're a lot cheaper. So cheap in fact, that it doesn't even pay us to make our own clothing anymore. It's cheaper to buy foreign made clothes off the rack. How can that be?

With all the costs along the production and supply chain how can something not ethically accreditedpossibly be produced for less than it costs to produce locally in New Zealand? The answer is simple: by exploiting workers.

In New Zealand the Tearfund and Baptist World Aid produce an Annual Ethical Fashion report where companies are assessed along the entire length of the supply chain from growers to packagers. In 2017 New Zealand companies included in the report were the following: Kowtow, Liminal Apparel, Karen Walker, Kathmandu, AS Colour, Glassons, Hallensteins, Barkers and Macpac.[1]Other global brands available in New Zealand that achieve the highest marks included: Zara, Bonds, Reebok, Adidas, Cotton On, Sheridan, Berlei, Jockey and Supre.[2]

Today fewer woollen garments are manufactured. They've given way to polyester and polypropylene. Unfortunately when these garments reach the end of their life and make their way to the dump the fibres do not biodegrade. They break down into smaller parts but they don't decompose to be taken up by the carbon or oxygen cycles. This is because they are plastic.

Polypropylene is the world's second most widely produced synthetic plastic after polyethylene. It is a thermoplastic polymer which means it comprises a series of molecules which become pliable when heated above a certain temperature. This means they will melt.

Buff is a Spanish company making headwear out of plastic drink bottles and Mac Pac use recycled plastic as insulation in jackets as an alternative to down. It's a good first step in addressing the plastic problem but we really can't just keep producing plastic because it never goes away. We look at this in chapter ten.

Panipat, ninety kilometres from Delhi, India, is home to a once thriving recycled wool industry. It was and still is the destination for the world's discarded wool garments but it is now a shadow of what it once was thanks to the demand for synthetic clothing.

In the early nineties the industry was worth some three hundred million dollars and employed hundreds of thousands of workers. Now it is worth only sixty two million dollars annually and employs sixty two thousand people. Its nearly two hundred wool recycling mills operate at half capacity. A number of factors combined to the industry's downturn: There was no investment in machinery able to deal with polypropylene, the costs of labour increased, the electricity supply was erratic and therefore could not be relied upon, machinery frequently broke down, business was fragmented and unregulated and the factory owners persisted with sweatshop conditions using child labour.[2]

As a minimalist you have the chance to think deeply about your clothing purchases. Once you become aware of where your clothes come from it is easier to refrain from purchasing them willy nilly. If you buy new clothes you have power to make sound and ethical financial decisions.

Coffee and Chocolate

Oil is the world's number one commodity and we saw how oil producing countries are the richest ones but not the happiest. Coffee is number two. The principal coffee bean growing nations are Brazil, Vietnam, Colombia, Indonesia and Ethiopia. So if all things are equal we would expect coffee growing nations to be wealthy. However, the converse is true. According to the International Monetary Fund's 2017 list of wealthy countries the above coffee growing countries are ranked as follows:

Brazil   81

Columbia   86

Indonesia	97
Vietnam	125
Ethiopia	166

Cocoa exporting countries don't fare any better. Ivory Coast, Ghana, Nigeria and Cameroon supply seventy percent of the world's cocoa beans.[3] These countries rank as follows on the 2017 International Monetary Fund rich country list:

Ivory Coast	143
Ghana	136
Nigeria	128
Cameroon	151

Now that you are aware of this you might think about it when you casually eat your next chocolate bar. You can help by purchasing chocolate with a fair trade label, but beware of the environmental cost: It takes an entire year's supply of cocoa beans from one tree to make a 450 gram cake of chocolate.

The competition between producers is intense and where producers are part of a cartel they have the means to drive the price down. This does two things: it makes the product more affordable to the consumer enticing her to use more and it squeezes the workers who work in the supply chain, so much so that after working in the fields all week they still don't have enough money to comfortably support their families.

It is estimated that 250 million child slaves are used in the production of coffee and cocoa[4]They are exposed to insecticides and fertilisers that are banned in other countries. Where workers are paid they have few rights and health and safety is not a priority for the plantation owners.

In the late 1980s the Fair Trade brand was established. Finally someone cared enough about the growers to do something about the conditions they endured. Suddenly on our shelves was coffee that pricked our conscience. It was organic and ethical. Now it's not only main stream, but it sits side by side with a myriad of other ethical coffees in large chain supermarkets.

Many coffee producers are members of the ISEAL Alliance which is a global association for members who adhere to credible sustainability standards. To be certified with the accreditation growers must adhere to the following practices:

- Sustainable principles;

- Wildlife conservation (locally);

- Minimising soil erosion (a problem in single crop agriculture);

- Treating workers fairly; and

- Maintaining clean water resources

If you don't see ethically produced coffee and chocolate in the mainstream aisle of the supermarket make sure you ask the supermarket to stock it, but also check out the organics or international aisles. Many good cafés also sell ethical coffee and chocolate.

Ethical Tea

When it comes to tea Fairtrade does not guarantee that workers get a much better deal than non-Fairtrade workers as most of the higher price for Fairtrade goods remains in the country where it is consumed.

The Ethical Tea Partnership was founded in 1997 to address human rights, labour and social issues, and to promote sustainability. Tea is a commodity that uses low paid tea pickers. Tea plantations have a reputation of using slave labour. This is because the pay is so low the pickers very easily get into debt to the company and effectively cannot leave. This can lead to the children of tea pickers being trafficked into domestic slavery on the promise of being provided with a job in a city. Children of tea pickers are often plucked out of school to assist the family meet their quota.

The Ethical Tea Partnership however does not focus strongly on human rights, with development and sustainability being the primary focus.

In India environmental initiatives have seen the development of an elephant corridor through the Sessa Tea Estate in Sonitpur. Working with the World Wildlife Fund tea plantation owners are mindful of the preservation of deer, rhino, elephants, leopards, migratory birds, hornbills, sloths, porcupines and striped neck mongoose. Gaurs, the largest species of wild cattle in the world, graze small patches of forest between tea plantations.

I have but scratched the social conscience surface but you get the idea. Ethical purchasing is a choice you can make for all the world's major commodities. You can support workers by purchasing fair trade goods and co-operative or boutique organic shops. These shops are great places to start. You might even find there is no need to use your local supermarket.

Importantly for you the consumer trying to de-clutter, there are some applications to be taken from this discussion:

- Research companies before you purchase

- Look for ethical accreditations

- Limit your purchasing to quality and be content to pay more for it

- Savour the purchase as though it will be the last one you'll buy

6

ART

"Manifest plainness, embrace simplicity, reduce selfishness, have few desires." Lao Tzu (Father of Taoism, 500BC)

What has art got to do with de-cluttering your house? Probably not a lot, but I want to illustrate that minimalism is not a new idea. Rather, it is a new application within consumerism. The idea of minimalist art and music possibly has always been around, since humans first scraped charcoal on a cave wall. I cover this topic to encourage you to stop and look around you. Is there a movement presently in the arts that is commenting on our excesses of consumption? Many artists presently incorporate recycled products into their work. Is this a form of minimalism?

Man has adorned his living space since he lived in caves. Paintings have been discovered on cave walls in Spain dating to 65,000 years before the present. That's about as old as art gets. This puts art in the hands of the Neanderthals. Other paintings found in caves in the Pilbara region of Western Australia and the Olary district of South Australia are estimated to be forty thousand years old. In Europe cave painters exploded onto the scene much later. Paintings have been discovered in Cauvet, France dating 32,000 to 30,000 years before the present, in Lascaux, France 17,000 years before the present and Altamira, Spain, 15,000 years before the present.

The images generally represent animals that shared the world with early humans. Sculptures too were part of early artistic expression, although probably as part of the spiritual culture, for instance statues of fertility goddesses or sun deities. Ever since then art has been subject to the prevailing fashion of the time, styles falling in and out of favour and undergoing re-invention as new generations rally against the establishment.

Art has always challenged convention. For much of our history artists have not been free to create as they like. Often the rulers of the day, a combination of the church and royalty, dictated what art was acceptable and if artists wanted a decent life they towed the line. If they fell out of favour they were exiled and probably died penniless. We only need to look back to the Nazi regime for a recent example of new works being labelled degenerate art. It is hard enough to make a living from art without the establishment putting the boot in. Plenty of artists have died misunderstood and destitute.

Throughout the last sixty thousand years humans replicated the world around them, depicted their interpretation of the gods and associated stories, represented heaven and earth, nobility and peasants, landscapes and portraits. Before World War I European painters explored the idea of capturing light in a movement called impressionism. This was followed by cubism which sought to distort the reality that the artist was faced with. It became mathematical and contrived. This in turn was followed by expressionism which sought to replace any semblance of realism with something that only conveyed emotion with the use of colour and line. Some remarkable painters emerged during the war. Such a talent was German expressionist Franz Marc whose young life ended in the battle of Verdun. His dear friend and co-founder of the Blue Rider art group, Paul Klee, only entered the war after his friend's death. One would think that art took a recess during the war but many artists did not fight.

The Great War changed everything. One hundred years ago there was a definitive change in art. It was as though a line had been drawn under the war. Nothing would be the same. Everything now was created as a reaction to the old society. Art, architecture and literature had a new canvas. No more arches and columns or dark canvases with gloomy interiors. The new style would embrace openness, as reflected in a new acceptance of a future peaceful and open society. Lines would be simple, clean. Colours would be limited. Designs would be stripped back to basic geometric forms. What does this sound like? A bit minimalist perhaps.

There emerged a school called Suprematism under the guidance of the Russian painter Kazmir Malevich. He was the master of innovation and a perfectly competent portraitist as evidenced by an impressionist style painting of "Flower Girl, 1903".But he abandoned this style, clearly satisfied at his accomplishments, to develop the intricate cubo-futurist style. His famous *The Knife Grinder* represented the industrial society that was taking off at the time. The painting is busy and calculated ,and the scene is a blur of frenetic activity as the knife grinder is swallowed by the action of the machine. It is a carefully orchestrated piece heavily influenced by the constructs of cubism. And it perfectly reflects the new industrial society. The viewer is forced to concentrate to fully interpret the painting.

At this time the war provided an opportunity and the necessity for invention. One of these was aerial photography. For the first time in human history the earth could be viewed from above. Imagine what they saw; a patchwork of fields coloured yellows and greens, grey stone walls, sinewy blue streaks of rivers reflecting the sun, dirt roads criss-crossing the landscape, trees as dark green dots.

The geometric forms of the landscape mesmerised Malevich. The simplicity of form entranced him. Prior to this his compositions were full of movement, mathematical finesse, even mysticism in the movement conveyed. Now he sought to represent the simplicity of the land and later of other subject matters, to reduce complexities right down to base components. As he did this his compositions became progressively simpler. We might view his work from the distance of one hundred years as simply a few irregular rectangles but not so. Malevich took a scene then reduced, reduced, reduced. He named this style Suprematist but he could just as well have named it minimalist. This was against a background of German expressionism which was vibrant, exciting and required no less studied concentration to interpret than Malevich's simple, carefully positioned, geometric shapes.

He famously unveiled his black square in the 1915 The Last Futurist (0.10) Exhibition in St Petersburg. This was the stake in the ground for abstract art. It didn't seek to represent anything. But its challenge, its provocativeness, was acutely understood. Malevich positioned the black square in the gallery in the corner, high up near the ceiling. This was where Russian religious icons were traditionally displayed. It was a deliberately mischievous act.

Malevich's Suprematist art had but one aim: to remove the self from nature and subject matter in order to achieve spirituality and supremacy of feeling. Compare this to Zen meditation. The two techniques appear to have the same aim.

But as with many new ideas that challenge the establishment, Malevich was not readily received by an adoring public. Undeterred, he produced a manifesto which sought to explain his art. At this time he also produced a series of *"White Square on White."* That requires little explanation.

Whilst Malevich had quite a following and was an inspiration for fellow artists, particularly in the decorative arts, he felt he had gone as far as he possibly could with Suprematist art. After all, to a reductionist, where could he go after such a seminal work? He was spent and went on to experiment with other styles. Malevich died as many geniuses before him died – penniless, misunderstood and unappreciated. It is only through looking with hindsight that history has judged him well.

Malevich's Suprematism Supremus No. 56, 1916.[1] Image retrieved from Wikimedia Commons. Public Domain.

Malevich's Black Square, 1915. [2] Image retrieved from Wikimedia Commons. Public Domain.

Malevich's White Square on White, 1917. [3] Image retrieved from Wikimedia Commons. Public Domain.

In the first quarter of the twentieth century a prominent movement emerged in the Netherlands. Theo van Doesburg and Piet Mondrian were instrumental in de Stijl, which translates as the Style. Van Doesburg was an art writer more than he was a painter and his vision was to create a new world order through the arts. It was to be a total rejection of what there was before the war. In 1917 he advertised through a journal he edited for like-minded artists to join him. Soon de Stijl comprised painters, poets, designers and architects.

Mondrian's Composition with Red, Yellow, Blue and Black, 1921. [4]
Image retrieved from Wikimedia Commons. Public Domain.

The main precepts of de Stijl were to reduce abstraction to its most basic tenents: line, form and colour. Lines were only ever used horizontally or vertically and colours were primary – yellow, red and blue. Form was balanced, not symmetrically, but by carefully positioned shapes and using voids and line. In order to reform society there was a need to eliminate distinctions between high art and applied art so furniture design and architecture readily exhibited de Stijl principles.

One hundred years on Mondrian's signature grid and primary colours can be seen in the Windows logo. Observe this next time your fire up your computer. Even modern font can be attributed to the de Stijl movement. There is a familiar typeface which is quite square. It is common in science fiction movies and analogue script. For this we can thank Theo van Doesburg and Richard Kegler.

Unsurprisingly there was an art movement call Minimalism. It was brief, although not as brief as Malevich's Suprematist art. The 1960s saw the new style emerge out of New York. This style was a reaction against the expressive art of the preceding decades which minimalists described as stale and academic.

Although the simplicity of minimalist works suggest, as Malevich prescribed, a release from the grip of emotion, this wasn't the primary aim of the 1960s minimalists. These works were a challenge to the concept that sculptures should be reverently displayed on a plinth and paintings hung on a wall. The artists refused to make their works aesthetically pleasing and used prefabricated materials such as plate steel and firebricks, assembling them in non-traditional settings such as galleries. For minimalists the idea was to present works where their own hands had not manipulated the materials. Thus the viewer was free to appreciate the form, which was often geometric, and the space around the form. Walking around the art, viewing it from all angles, experiencing the weight and height, was an essential interaction in appreciating this new art.

Minimalist art had no appetite for emotion, symbolism or emotional content and in this regard it compares with Suprematist art. But surely the act of experiencing the art, which is designed to be confronting, one must feel something, even something as fundamental as a like or dislike of it.

Surprisingly the major influences on the 1960s minimalist movement derived from the Dutch de Stijl group, the Russian Constructivists and the German Bauhaus, all of which had exhibited work in New York.

The constructivist approach utilised modular construction and industrial materials in place of traditional sculpting mediums. The use of such methods provided anonymity of the artist which was an aim of the style. The traditional notions of sculpture were thus challenged and lines between traditional mediums blurred.

Frank Stella was a minimalist pioneer. In 1959 he produced a provocatively named black painting called *Ore Fahne Hock! (Raise the Flag High)*, a Nazi reference. It is monochromatic, matt, unframed and flat. It has a pinstripe pattern which invites the viewer to scrutinise. This painting was part of a series of Black Paintings that Stella produced 1958-1960 and which made him famous by the age of twenty three. Explaining the works Stella said, 'What you see is what you see,' which became the movement's mantra. The work is challenging, at once repelling the viewer with its harshness and repugnant title but at the same time compelling as the viewer is drawn in close to make something of the stripes. It can be found in the Whitney Museum of American Art. Interestingly forty five years had passed since Malevich's *Black Square*. Malevich and Stellas' rebellions culminated in almost identical artworks.

Tony Smith presented *Die* in 1962. He carefully considered the scale of his six foot rolled half inch steel cube. Its dimensions needed to relate to the human body. Any smaller and the cube would be viewed merely as an object. Any larger would render it a monument. Weighing two hundred and twenty six kilograms it rested on the gallery floor as if left over from a building site. It was everything minimalist art represented: visually unappealing and hostile. The title is ambiguous. In essence it is a six foot box and this could reference the title. But the box is also die cast. The viewer is invited to consider the wordplay. It is housed in the National Gallery of Art in Washington DC.

Carl Andre used a row of industrial firebricks in 1966 to challenge viewers' relationship with art. Called *Lever*, it resembled a fallen column as it projected from the wall across the gallery floor. Again, there was no manipulation by the hand of the artist. It is the choice of every day industrial objects contrived into a form, in this case a row, set in a public art gallery that challenged the notion of art. Any reverence was abandoned, finesse and aesthetic value ignored. Andre was provocative. Describing himself as the Turner of matter, Turner who severed colour from depictions. As to himself, he attempted to sever matter from depiction. What does he mean? He considered wood as the "mother of matter" and bricklayers as people of fine craft.

The cube was a popular form in the minimalist era. It featured again when Robert Morris constructed four mirrored cubes between 1965 and 1971. They sit in the gallery space; cold, challenging, as if they've been scattered by a giant playing a game. Prior to this Morris had created large grey plywood boxes for a ballet set. The mirrored cubes invite the viewer to be part of the art as they see themselves within it.

Untitled by Donald Judd in 1969 challenged the traditional way art was viewed by presenting several framed canvases hanging horizontally out from the wall one above the other. The use of repeated identical shapes and the lack of a name for the work emphasises the minimalist ethos of freedom from emotion and lack of reverence. This work is found in Hirshhorn Museum and Sculpture Garden, Washington DC. Judd created a series of this work, always on the same scale but never the same colours. His work existed in three-dimensional space and blurred the lines between painting and sculpture. Hanging on the wall like a painting but clearly sculptural, Judd rejected traditions such as the use of a plinth. The lack of a title emphasises the minimalist ethos of distancing the artist from the work.

Richard Serra, in 1969, also worked on the cube, but this time he deconstructed it in *One Ton Prop (House of Cards)*. Without a top or bottom the four two hundred and twenty six kilogram slabs of steel rest on each other for support. While each side in practice leans securely on another, to remove one side would result in the entire piece collapsing. Again, the viewer must walk around it and contemplate what makes it art. It can be found in the MoMA, New York.

Ronald Baden's work was a little atypical of mainstream minimalism in that he employed diagonal lines. However, that is the main digression. In all other respects he was a minimalist; he used industrial materials and left surfaces unfinished. In 1966 he created a giant cast steel X.

Finally we cross the Atlantic to the Tate Gallery, London. Here can be viewed *Two Open Modular Cubes/Half-Off* 1973 by Sol LeWitt. Sol famously said "the most interesting characteristic of the cube is that it is relatively uninteresting." His specialty was repeated geometric form, lacking in colour. The modular nature of the open cubes could be used in repeated patterns. The titles of his works suggest one can visualise the works without even viewing them to know what they comprise. This was perfect minimalist theory. The title of the works and the works themselves provoked no emotion and exhibited no beauty.

Photography

One can furnish a room very luxuriously by taking furniture out rather than putting it in." Francis Jourdain (1876-1958) Furniture maker, interior designer, painter

It is interesting that minimalist photography as artistic expression did not find its place in 1960s New York. The world had to wait until at least the mid seventies before anything remotely minimalist appeared. The main proponents were born in the 1940s and 1950s.

Adopting the same reductive processes as for painting and sculpture the artist stripped away what was not important leaving the viewer's entire focus on the subject matter. Colour was used as a tool to make up for limited subject matter, either in a complementary or a contrasting manner. A recurring pattern with the works is another prevalent theme such as strong vertical or horizontal lines. These make for particularly bold compositions.

The aim was to capture the essence of the subject and to this end sometimes a texture could take the place of an obvious subject. Let's meet some of the artists and see how they achieved their minimalist style.

Germany's Andreas Gursky produced oversized architecture and landscape photographs in colour. Some of these works measured two by three metres. Gursky employed an elevated vantage point and his favoured subjects were large, anonymous man-made spaces such as stock exchanges, high rise facades at night and the interiors of big box retailers. It seems that organised chaos might be one of the attractions as these scenes are full of colour and interest. However, grid structures provide order and a sense of grounding.

Of his work Gursky says it reflects anonymous beat-heavy music with its symmetry and simplicity while playing towards a more visceral emotion. His 1999 photograph *99 Cents Only Store* certainly echoes the former part of the statement. The shelves extend across the frame and contain stripes of coloured packets. The shop is precise and orderly, the viewer's eye not fixed on any particular subject. As to the visceral emotion, each viewer will know if Gursky has achieved his aim.

Another big box store photograph, *Amazon 2016*, also features strong horizontal lines which span the entire frame. This time there are no colour groups as the books appear to be in complete chaos, like a flower market. However, other strong structural components are evident: three russet brown columns in the background and a white grid suspended ceiling. These big box works certainly employ the use of the minimalists' favourite shapes.

Michael Kenna from the United Kingdom is noted for his stunning black and white landscapes. Ethereal light is achieved through ten hour long exposures at dawn and dusk. The result is stark simplicity which appears ghostly, never stark or harsh. He might photograph a tree with a background of a field or a hill. Detail is lost but form, line and tone are paramount. The work is always intelligent, composed, evocative and supremely captivating.

Kenna has travelled the world photographing landscapes. A New Zealand photograph entitled *Eastlands, New Zealand 2014* comprises an arc of a star cluster as the stars move across the night sky. This was achieved by an eleven hour long exposure. Below this is a simple landscape in silhouette.

From the natural world to the built environment, American Grant Hamilton came to photography from a graphic design background. He says his aim is to find beauty in the mundane and this is achieved by highlighting the obvious that people never noticed before.

Hamilton's work is colourful but intensely simple. There might be two or three blocks of colour which make up the entire frame. His subject matter is ubiquitous: signs and buses provide the props. In 2006 he began using a Polaroid SX-70 camera which produced square images. He loved this medium; the square format suited his subject matter and the fact that there were no negatives was especially appealing. The subject matter is unrecognisable in Hamilton's finished pieces as he engages so closely with it. Artistic merit lies in the form, line and flat colour.It is only a matter of time until Hamilton exhausts his supply of Polaroid film. Interesting times ahead.

Hirosho Sugimoto trained as an architect and moved from Tokyo to New York in 1974. His photos are a series of events in times and Sugimoto likens the practice to a time capsule. He focuses on the transience of life and the conflict between life and death.

There is much use of black and white in his work and he also employs long exposure techniques. An early series was shot entirely within a natural history museum in black and white. Dioramas of bygone eras are represented as if the viewer were actually back in time seeing it with their own eyes.

Sugimoto says his influences are Marcel Duchamp and the art movements Dadaism and Surrealism. This is interesting in that these short-lived but fascinating movements embraced an anti-art philosophy in the case of Dadaism and dreams over reality in the case of Surrealism. Certainly these styles are fun and don't appear to have the same ideals as Sugimoto. In trying to compare his work with the above I also fall short. For example Sugimoto's series on seascapes is two dimensional and meditative, a far cry from the mad-cap works associated with the above movements.

American photographer Peter Downsbrough moved to Brussels in 1989 at the age of forty nine. His photographs don't reflect nature or the built environment. Rather, he composes what he photographs. Trained as an architect, he has worked extensively with the straight line. A black straight line, to be precise. Often it is adhered to or painted onto a plain white wall. However, it has also been suspended in gallery space. The line is usually horizontal or vertical, not diagonal or bent or curved. Added to the line he arranges small black lower case letters into the simplest of words. These are small conjunctive words such as and, if, but, and then. He explains that the grammar invites the viewer to jump from one thought to another. Downsbrough's work is certainly minimalist. It is cold, calculated and precise. It is not aesthetically pleasing.

Hans Hilterman from the Netherlands came to the minimalist genre of photography through his work as an advertising photographer where one image has to convey a story. His most notable work is the *You* series where Hilterman captures over one thousand human portraits. They are not just any portrait. Stripped of adornment, make-up and expression, the sitters are meditative, their guard let down. They look at the viewer as they would a family member which translates to you, the viewer.

In recent years there has been a resurgence in black and white photography. It seems to have the effect of drawing the viewer in as if there is a need to search out every nook and cranny. Black and white photography is full of mystery.

Today everyone is a photographer thanks to mobile phones. We wait with bated breath to see what artists can do with this ubiquitous medium.

7

MUSIC

"Wealth is not in having vast riches, it is in contentment."
Muhammed (570-632CE), Founder of Islam

It should come as no surprise that there is a genre of music that is minimalist and like all art forms it developed as a counter to the preceding genres. The art movement in 1960s New York provided the platform on which to experiment with minimalist music. Some major players emerged: Steve Reich, Philip Glass, Terry Riley, La Monte Young and John Adams.

The music was bold, simple and repetitive but to achieve this simplicity many new techniques were employed in a single piece of work which could be hours in duration. The idea was to strip down music by limiting notes or instruments. Some pieces comprise endless circles, others are underlain by a drone throughout the entire piece. Many instruments were used including voice and found objects such as drinking glasses.

The style is marked by a lack of direction in the Western sense of music. It doesn't seem to have a goal. One section follows on from another, although the sections are not disjointed. Minimalist music is an uninterrupted flow of interlocking rhythmic pulses and patterns. But it is far from dull as it employs brightness of sounds which are manipulated as they are repeated. As a listener it is fun to listen to a work and predict a technique. This is important as one of the goals of minimalist music is to challenge the listener to listen in a new way by focussing on the internal process of the music. This is a similar goal of minimalist art where the interaction of the viewer was integral to the art experience.

Compositions typically limit notes to a short rif or melody which are then expanded or contracted, sped up or slowed down. These can be repeated in loops under which other passages are played or sung. Notes within the melody can change one note at a time over a repeated melody. This is a technique called metamorphosis. A major work by Philip Glass is titled Metamorphosis. Another technique is static harmony where a chord is changed into another chord gradually. And then there is accenting one note in the melody so over a number of phrases that note tends to take on a rhythm across the melody. This is called rhythmic displacement. A tricky idea is that of phasing. This is having a slightly longer or shorter version of the melody which is repeated until it becomes synchronised with the original timing of that melody. Underneath all of that is often employed a long drone note which is held or repeated throughout. Repeated notes throughout can also act as a drone.

A breakthrough in the genre came in 1976 with Steve Reich's "Music for 18 Musicians." The piece is over one hour long and features percussion in the form of xylophones and a shaker, as well as a clarinet, violin, cello, piano, and four voices. The viewer is mesmerised by the performance. In fact when minimalist music first evolved it was give the name hypnotic music. It is like that. It's addictive. There is enough there to keep your attention and you can't quite put your finger on what it is. Where a Beethoven symphony washes over the listener, enveloping her in a complex array of melodies and counter-melodies, the minimalist piece burrows inside her to make her feel as though she's part of the music-making process. It is utterly impossible to pull oneself away from the performance.

A key element to the performance of minimalist music is the attention given to the setting. The backdrop might be a series of vertical lines to give emphasis to the repetitive music or it could be matt black, so long as it enhances the experience of the music.

The only way to understand minimalist music is to listen to it. Below is a summary of the abovementioned composers and a discussion on the seminal works from each. I urge you to explore this amazing genre.

Steve Reich, born 1936

What a trailblazer this man was. A true master must be thoroughly competent and cognizant of classical theory in order to pare the music back to its simplest form. This idea is the musical version of Picasso's statement "It's taken me a lifetime to learn to paint like a child."

Against a background of the minimalist art scene in 1960s New York, Reich founded his own ensemble and explored aspects of Classical Western music as well as the patterns and structures of non-western music and jazz. Reich immersed himself in African studies, Balinese, Indonesian Gamelan and traditional forms of cantillation (chanting) of the Hebrew scriptures. Early works such as *It's Gonna Rain* and *Come Out* are marked by repetitive structures and slow harmonic rhythms. These pieces aren't easy to listen to as Reich uses taped loops of the human voice to single out notes but the innovation and genius has to be admired.

The 1988 work, *Different Trains*, I similarly find difficult to listen to, but as with all types of minimalist music, I find that it draws me in, the repetitive structures enveloping me in its hypnosis.

Reich has been awarded multiple prizes including the 2009 Pulitzer Prize in Music for his composition *Double Sextet*. It is a wind and strings piece in which Reich used a tape of the ensemble to play over the original work. Thus, the one flute, one cello, one piano, one xylophone, one violin and one clarinet becomes two flutes, two cellos, two pianos, two xylophones, two violins and two clarinets. The flute and clarinet play long notes with no discernable melody, the structures are repetitive and the percussion is bright. It is relatively short at around twenty minutes.

Philip Glass, born 1937

Glass is a minimalist composer genius but his lifetime output is far from minimal. Since the 1960s Glass has been a collaborative musician and composer working with rock, pop and non-Western artists. In 1967 he founded the Philip Glass ensemble after working and studying in Europe.

Glass's repertoire is extensive. He can claim twenty five operas, twelve symphonies, three piano concertos, fifty three movie sound tracks as well as scores for voice, chorus, theatre, dance, quartets and television. His compositions for the films, *Kandun*, *The Hours* and *Notes on a Scandal* received Oscar nominations. It is The Hours music that captures me. Utterly beautiful, simple, haunting. You will recognise Glass's works even if you are not aware that he was the composer.

One of the most stunning pieces of work is the opera *Einstein on the Beach* in which he collaborated with Robert Wilson. The opera is four hours thirty minutes long, has no interval, no plot and conceivably no link between words, images and music. It challenged the opera world in 1976 because it doesn't tell a story at all. Rather it explores the idea of Einstein, the character of the man. In this work dancers are the principals and they are dressed in muted tones so as to merge with the stage props. Visually it is dark, with the stage lights highlighting the odd piece of white clothing. Perhaps to call this work opera is a stretch, but opera derives from the word opus which means work. It is a magnificent piece of work, a feat of endurance for the actors, dancers and musicians, as well as the audience. The work achieves the aim of engaging the listener or viewer in a new way. There is the familiar drone undercurrent, urgent and repetitive, which provides energy and continuity. The singers use words in a similar fashion, merely repeating simple phrases, or numbers. It is never boring and always surprising.

Terry Riley, born 1935

Riley's early introduction to Indian classical music and jazz influenced his compositions. He even taught Indian music.

His best known and seminal piece is the 1964 *In C* in which fifty three fragments can be played by any number and combinations of players and instruments and at any speed. This was a ground-breaking, highly influential work. Choppy and repetitive high piano notes lead to overlays of a carefully orchestrated cacophony which settles, as the ear becomes accustomed, to a series of each instrument's own patterns. It feels chaotic, almost as if the orchestra is tuning up. However, there is obvious composition as one instrument plays against another and it is fun to listen acutely for these patterns. The high piano chopping never lets up which keeps the energy high.

This is an exercise in listening to music. You can't have it on in the background while you do something else. It is mesmerising to watch and it takes as much concentration to listen and to watch as it does the musicians to play it. If it was performed live I would go to see it.

His 1969 album *Rainbow in Curved Air* followed and this became a landmark in minimalist music. The eastern music, western avant-garde and jazz are all evident, with droning, sustained organ, controlled blasts of saxophone and shimmering repeating melody patterns.

Riley composed seven film scores as well as the soundtrack for the video game Grand Theft Auto IV. In 1977 he released *Descending Moonshine Dervishes* which came after studies with Indian musicians. Soft long-held drone notes with rapidly repeating overlays give the work an electronic feel. It is a departure from Reich's and Glass's percussive feel. *Rainbow in Curved Air* has the feel of being in a computer games arcade with its unexpected bright patterns over a droning rhythm.

It is recognised that it was Riley's work that influenced Mike Oldfield's Tubular Bells (1973). And that without that platform Tubular Bells may not have had the acceptance that it did have.

La Monte Young, born 1935

Young was a pioneer of Western drone music, which originally went by the term dream music. Arriving in New York from California in 1960 with an interest in Eastern music he found the perfect environment in which to explore and develop the new minimalist music. He was influenced by Gregorian Chant, Indian classical music, Indonesian gamelan music and jazz. Early works include the twelve tone technique which was derived by Arnold Schoenberg where all twelve notes are given equal importance and thus there is no key. Young says he was influenced from an early age by continuous sounds such as the wind blowing on the house and the transformer hum on telephone poles.

In 1964 he conceived of a piece called *The Well-Tuned Piano* which was originally released only on tape. An evolving piece, he finally performed it in 1975. It is based on mathematics and Hindustani classical music and is over six hours long. In this work it would appear that silence is as important as the sound the notes make. The work is directionless and restful.

Young influenced JJ Cale's Velvet Underground, Brian Eno, Andy Warhol and Lou Reed.

John Adams, born 1947

Born a decade after the previous minimalist composers Adams cannot be slotted into a strict minimalist genre. You might recognise his work for which he won the Pulitzer Prize in Music in 2003 for composing the choral work *On the Transmigration of Souls* which was commissioned by the New York Philharmonic to commemorate the first anniversary of 9/11. The piece begins with police and fire sirens in the distance until voices come in repeating names. You need to concentrate as this is barely audible. These all seem to be on a looped background. Over this are smooth high voices interspersed with musical notes until the singers chant the word remember. The music feels heavenly and dark at the same time. It then becomes urgent and guttural rising to crescendos and falling off again like waves. There is no accompanying video to this piece of music.

Adams uses significant events as themes for his operas and other works. I first came across his music when I attended the opera *Nixon in China* which he composed in 1987. The music captivated me. It was urgent, constant and energetic. I had not been exposed to such a style before. I was hooked. I can look back at every opera I have seen and *Nixon in China* is right at the top of my favourites, and this from someone who does not like English speaking operas. It is the music.

Other operas by Adams include *Dr Atomic* (2005), *Short Ride in a Fast Machine* (1986) and *Death of Klinghoffer* (1991). His seminal work however is a series of repeating loops of oscillations on string instruments called *Shaker Loops* composed in 1978. Relatively short at twenty six minutes, the work relies on strings to imitate the sound of water, shimmering, shuddering and shaking. It is a series of modular components in four movements: shaking and trembling, hymning slews, loops and verses and finally, a final shaking. The first movement featured nine years later in the movie Barfly and the first three movements are part of the soundtrack to a video game called Civilization IV.

In summary this chapter has been about bringing to our attention minimalists movements in recent times. It is fascinating to explore and to try to understand what each group was trying to achieve.

8

ARCHITECTURE

"Make things as simple as possible but no simpler." Albert Einstein
1879

I have to include architecture in any discourse on minimalism, for it gives us the glorious phrase "less is more." In terms of architecture design, less is more expensive. Clean lines, simple structures. Such aesthetics require more design and engineering input than current popular architecture and are thus more expensive to create.

The aim of minimal architecture is to utilise fewer elements to achieve strong design. It relies upon simplicity, restraint of colour, detail and form. With the intense desire to present something simple comes the challenge to achieve warmth, especially when designing dwellings.

This simplicity is achieved by smooth or uncomplicated wall claddings and wall linings. Alternately repetitive texture or a strong pattern can equally provide uncluttered simplicity.

Careful attention to light is paramount as it can provide interest in a plain space where detailing is absent. A key effect of minimal architecture is open space, or voids which welcome light. One architect took this concept to the extreme. Self-taught Japanese designer Tadao Ando, in 1976, designed the Row House, or Azuma House in Osaka. This multi-level dwelling has no exterior windows, and nestled between two traditional timber apartments, looks like a concrete shoe box with the short side to the street. But Ando was a genius. Using the rule of thirds, he divided the space into three and removed the central portion. He opened the house up to the sky! In other words he removed the roof of the central third of the dwelling. The occupants were totally exposed to the heavens, with light infiltrating all rooms except the bathroom. It meant, however, that if they needed the bathroom and it was raining, they'd need an umbrella because it was located away from the living areas.

Without windows the occupants could feel like they were anywhere in the world. And that's what Ando wanted.

Tadao Ando's Row House or Azuma House. Image retrieved from Wikimedia Commons. Author Oiuysdfg. [1]

Ando has culture and tradition on his side. It should come as no surprise that a son of Zen or ma should create the earliest and most stunning example of a minimalist house. Ando's early years however, were influenced by the American architect Frank Lloyd Wright who had designed the Imperial Hotel in Tokyo. Ando saw this building as a teenager and was so moved by it, he abandoned his promising career as a boxer and began to study design.

Ando employs clever use of empty space which in Zen philosophy represents the beauty of simplicity. He utilises concrete as a medium more than anything else as it is clean and gives simple lines and strength without looking cumbersome.

His treatment of dwelling houses and churches is exactly the same, with his ethos that a dwelling has a spiritual heart. He utilises natural light and designs structures to follow the natural lie of the land rather than destroy the landscape to accommodate a building.

Ando is an architect who was part of a continuum of innovation in design. He could not have achieved the success without the movements that came before him. We need to understand what was happening post World War 1, particularly in Europe.

A handful of visionary architects and designers became prominent after the war, embracing new technologies and construction techniques as part of the new social order. Working in Europe was Walter Gropius and Ludwig Mies van der Rohe in Germany, JJP Oud in Holland, Philip Johnson in the United States and Le Corbusier and Gerrit-Rietveld in France.

One style in particular enjoyed a short duration but nevertheless influenced the architecture that followed. Between 1917 and 1931 the de Stijl movement encompassed a new minimalist art and architecture. Translated as 'the style', it was also known as Neoplasticism. It developed in response to the horrors of World War 1 and the desire to rebuild society with an emphasis on the individual. The social aspiration at this time was to use art and architecture to remove the individualism of the artist in favour of precision and universal harmonies. Its proponents believed they were laying the groundwork for a new future utopia.

Artist Piet Mondrian, architect JJP Oud and arts writer Theo Van Doesburg were the founding members and driving force of the movement. Pared down, abstract geometric forms and primary colours signify the de Stijl aesthetic. The principal idea was to ignore the natural forms of nature and colour. Asymmetry was also key and paintings or buildings would achieve balance by the use of opposition. A carefully positioned post or support might be all that is required to resolve the asymmetry. Vertical and horizontal lines are positioned in planes that don't intersect to give the feeling that each element exists independently. This is demonstrated beautifully in the Rietveld Schroder House and the Red Blue Chair designed by Gerrit-Rietveld.

The Rietveld Schroder House. Image retrieved from Wikimedia Commons. Author Andreas 2309. [2]

Rietveld Schroder House is the only true de Stijl dwelling ever built. Located in Utrecht, it was constructed in 1924, having been commissioned by Mrs Truus Schroder-Schrader for herself and her three children. She asked that it be built without walls as a commitment to a new openness about relationships within families and to the truth within their emotional lives.

Situated on the end of a row of terrace houses, no attempt was made to aesthetically fit the dwelling in with the houses around it. Starkly contrasted, it consists of a series of planes, posts and windows where ninety degrees is a paramount design feature. It has no symmetry and balance is achieved between solid and empty space as well as the use of the grid. Little distinction is made between the interior and exterior space with the use of grey and white surfaces, and black window and door frames. The interior makes uses of sliding walls so spaces can be transformed for different uses. The quintessential de Stijl features of the dwelling are the vertical and horizontal posts and beams which are painted in red and yellow. Mrs Schroder-Shrader lived there until 1985. It is now a museum and listed as a World Heritage site.

The idea of forms existing in their own planes is none more evident than in Gerrit-Rietveld's Red Blue Chair which was designed in 1918. It comprises a blue rectangular piece of wood as the seat, a red rectangular piece of wood as the chair back, and highly lacquered black timber legs, arms and cross-members. At the ends of each support is a tell-tale feature that screams de Stijl: yellow. The yellow squares complete the primary colour triad.

Rietveld's Red Blue Chair. Image retrieved from Wikimedia Commons. Author Sailko. [3]

The de Stijl movement drew heavily on Cubism and it in turn influenced the German Art School, the Bauhaus, which helped give rise to the International Style which was predominant in the 1920s and 1930s. The Bauhaus School Building in Dessau, Germany, was designed by Walter Gropius in 1925 to house the German Art School.

However, it only served the school until 1932 before it was forced to close under pressure from the emerging Nazi regime. It is an iconic example of the International Style with its strong rectangular form, muted colour palette and striking use of glass curtain wall cladding.

The building is a series of structures laid out in an asymmetric pinwheel. Three wings provide space for student accommodation and teaching rooms whilst a two level connecting bridge provides administration space. In true International Style, the four level rectangular building has a glass curtain wall to the outsides of the upper three floors. Only the ground floor has obvious concrete wall divisions. A white concrete ledge separates the ground floor from those above it. Attached to this building's end is a flattened cigarette packet shaped structure with the word Bauhaus running down it in bold white lettering.

The building stands starkly on its site completely unadorned by decoration. Painted in a limited palette of grey and white, one red door at ground level suggests understated and undeniable International Style. Surrounding the buildings are pale grey paths that lie at ninety degrees to any wall and these frame large squares of tidy green grass.

Achievements in stunning simplicity, the buildings were designed to reflect the school's design philosophy of promoting a unified vision for the arts that made no distinction between form and function. The school became a UNESCO World Heritage site in 1996.

Groupius's Bauhaus School, 1926. Image retrieved from Wikimedia Commons. Author Lannguyen138 [4]

Gropius's Bauhaus School, 1926. Author M_H.DE. [5]

While Germany was coming to terms with the new building styles a Swiss designer in France was upsetting the establishment. In 1925 Le Corbusier designed a building for the Paris Exhibition of Modern and Decorative Industrial Art, later to be known as Art Deco. His L'Espirit Nouveau Pavilion was a radical departure from the decorative architecture of the time. The site he was allotted contained trees which were not to be felled so he simply incorporated a tree into his dwelling.

Le Corbusier's L'Espirit Nouveau Pavilion, 1925. Image retrieved from Wikimedia Commons. Author SiefkinDR [6]

Le Corbusier was obsessed with the mechanisation of construction so it would be fair to assume that his design emphasis was always going to be on the industrial concept of the decorative arts.

Part of the brief for this project was to design a dwelling for a city of three million people. Le Corbusier thought of the building as a cell extracted from a large apartment building and chose materials which were mass produced and therefore freely available. Its design eschewed ornamentation and adhered to the International Style principles. Rectangular in shape, it comprised open spaces, ninety degree angles to the planes, a flat roof and built in furniture. The organisers of the exhibition were furious. But time has a way of altering perception. Le Corbusier had such a significant effect on modern architecture that in 2016 seventeen of his projects in seven countries were designated UNESCO World Heritage sites.

Le Corbusier is well known for a dwelling he designed in Poissy, France in 1929. The Villa Savoye resembles a chocolate box resting on a column with a ship's round squat smokestack and various other rectangles on top. The building is constructed from reinforced concrete and is flat white. No gardens surround it, only flats of green grass. It is interesting that Le Corbusier used a curve and is one of the few International Style designers to do so. He was also a proponent of the use of modular proportions in order to maintain a human scale in the work. The State purchased Villa Savoye in 1958 and is a UNESCO World Heritage site.

Le Corbusier's 1929 Villa Savoye. Image retrieved from flickr user YoGomi [7]

Although he appeared to follow the design principles of other architects working at the time, he produced his own five point manifesto. The first point was that supporting walls should be replaced by a grid of reinforced concrete columns. The second that there should be free design of the ground plan and the free design of the façade to enable the exterior of the building to separate from its structural design is the third. The use of ribbon windows is the fourth and the last point concerns the dual function of the flat roof.

Oud was working as the Municipal Housing Architect in Rotterdam when he designed apartments for the part of the Weissenhof Estate as part of the 1927 Deutscher Werkbund Exhibition in Stuttgart. The project was led by Mies and comprised twenty-one buildings that contained sixty dwellings. Seventeen architects collaborated on the project and a common theme developed; the International Style. All but two of the entries were white, they had simple but striking facades, flat roofs used as terraces and open plan interiors.

Oud designed a row of five two storey concrete stucco apartments with gardens at the rear. Each apartment comprises more than four exterior walls with other rectangular protrusions added to create interest. The black window bands are all the detail allowed and these are echoed at the roof line. Stunning and simple. To one end is a garden wall where two planes meet at a curved intersect. Each unit comprises a full bathroom and three bedrooms upstairs with the kitchen and living areas downstairs.

It was important to Oud that the building be constructed in materials fashioned from machines, for to him, at that time, machines were able to give more plastic expression than the hand. Also important was the affordability factor that mass production enabled.

Oud's Weissenhof Estate apartments, 1927. Photo shows the back of the apartments. Image retrieved from Wikimedia Commons. Author Andreas Praefcke. [8]

Unfortunately due to damage incurred during World War II, only eleven buildings of the Weissenhof Estate survive, the above-described Oud apartment block being one of the survivors. It is a UNESCO World Heritage site.

Ludwig Mies van der Rohe (1886-1969) was a proponent of the new order of post World War 1 where anything associated with the old world was to be shunned. His part in designing buildings as well as the furniture that went in them was his way of providing the new social order something to lay a foundation on. Ornamentation was abandoned, and like the de Stijl movement, the emphasis was on simple geometric forms, clean lines, pure colour and an extension of space around and beyond the interior walls. Mies referred to his buildings as skin and bone architecture.

Whilst working in Germany he was commissioned to design the German Pavilion for the 1929 Barcelona Exhibition. Stunningly elegant, the building is a classic example of the simplicity of free plan architecture where space is open plan with non-load bearing walls used to divide the space.

The building has planes which comply to the ninety degree principle, its shape being rectangular with a flat roof. Constructed on a slab of travertine, the slab extends beyond the building to project out over a pool which visually connects the interior with the exterior.

Inside, steel columns are interspersed with freely spaced planes. There were no exhibits to speak of inside the pavilion. The building itself was exhibit enough with its stunning use of red onyx, marble and travertine, all hugely expensive and lavish materials. The design of the interior space, and indeed the location of the pavilion within the exhibition grounds channelled the visitor through it to the exhibition's most popular attraction, the Poble Espanyol. Mies's aim was to create a space of tranquillity for visitors. There was but one item of interest not connected to the building; a chair especially designed by Mies which became known as the exhibition chair. The German Pavilion was deconstructed in 1930 as was expected for the temporary exhibit. However, in 1983-1986 it was reconstructed.

Mies' German Pavilion for the 1929 Barcelona Exhibition. Image retrieved from Wikimedia Commons. Author "© Alice Wiegand / CC BY-SA 3.0 (via Wikimedia Commons)". [9]

In 1930 Mies was commissioned by the Tugendhats to design a dwelling in the fashionable Brno district of the now Czech Republic. This building also attracted critical acclaim. Constructed on a hillside, the main entrance is situated at street level and this floor is all the passerby can observe. The other two levels float down the hill behind like a waterfall.

Again, the design is sleek, rectangular and beautifully simple. It is constructed from reinforced concrete over an iron frame. The floor area is generous for the time, incorporating the nanny's flat and ancillary associated spaces. The strength of the construction allowed supporting walls to be dispensed with. The interior therefore could be arranged to maximise space and light. One wall is a sheet of plate glass that descends into the basement as a car window would descend into the door frame.

Colour palette is limited to muted whites and creams with the onyx providing warm colours. There are no paintings or ornamentation of any kind. Mies and an interior design collaborator, Lilly Reich, designed cantilevered slat back chairs with squabs in red, green and white. This is enough colour for the space and complements the abundant potted shrubs located in the patios and which are viewed from the living spaces. These two styles of chair are even made today and are known as the Tugendhat and Brno chairs.

The Tugendhat dwelling is an icon of modernism architecture. After various uses during and since World War II it became a museum in 1994.

Mies' Tugendhat House in Czech Republic, 1930. Rear view. Image retrieved from Wikimedia Commons. Author Daniel Fišer (-df-). [10]

Mies' Tugendhat House. Upper level. Image retrieved from Wikimedia Commons. Author Rory Hyde. [11]

Mies' friend Walter Gropius arrived in the United States in 1937 to take a teaching position at Harvard University's Graduate School of Design in Massachusetts. He immediately designed Gropius House for his family and subsequently used it as an example for his students. Situated on five acres, it was designed to have the critical outdoor flow. To that end Gropius transplanted trees to create the right landscape for the house.

The flat roof design suggests an almost Japanese quality as the house nestles against mature broad-branching trees and is framed by low stone walls. Everywhere ninety degree planes are evident as is the use of vertical railings and supports. Gropius not only used the signature concrete, glass and steel but incorporated local timbers, clapboards, plaster and bricks.

The interior adhered to International Style design principles of openness and light and comprises a living area open to the dining room. In the less sunlit corner of the house are no less than four bathrooms. Gropius's wife lived there after his death in 1969, and in 1985, one year after her death, it became a museum. In 2002 Gropius House was designated a National Historic Landmark.

Gropius House, 1938, Massachusetts. Image retrieved from Wikimedia Commons. Author <u>Daderot</u>. [12]

Gropius House, Massachusetts. Side view. Image retrieved from Wikimedia Commons. Author Magicpiano. [13]

International Style was a term coined by Philip Johnson and Henry-Russell Hitchcock who curated an architectural exhibition in the Museum of Modern Art in 1932. Common themes were obvious throughout the buildings they chose. Rectangular forms were dominant, the buildings having flat roofs, without a gable in sight. This was a practical aspect of the style, with roof gardens able to be useful for the occupiers and as protection for the concrete roof.

Expansive planes were utilised, unadorned. All ornamentation was spurned as belonging to the old world order. Interior spaces were open and often had the ability to be reconfigured. The buildings seemed to float as there were no unwieldy columns bearing the weight of floors, rather, cantilevered planes were used with the modern building materials.

Philip Johnson cemented his place in International Style architecture when he designed and built the Glass House in New Canaan, Connecticut. The property was his and comprised forty seven acres. He was tireless in his treatment of the site to ensure it complemented not only the Glass House but also the fourteen structures he built on the property over the next fifty years.

The glass house is literally a 166 square metre rectangle with floor to ceiling glass walls fixed between black steel struts and H-beams. These panes are five and a half metres wide so the space feels seamless. A point of interest is a cylindrical brick room one third along inside the dwelling. This extends a short distance beyond the roof. Naturally it houses the bathroom, but on the living area side of the bathroom is an open fireplace and a timber half wall. The floor is lined with dark tan bricks in herringbone pattern.

The glass provides ever-changing interest as sunlight and shadow enter the space, trees cast shadows and even the occupants add layers of shadow.

Surrounding the dwelling are low stone walls and flat expanses of grass. The Connecticut woods serve as a backdrop. Quite near, but not so close as to spoil the effect of the Glass House, is a brick guest house. Deliberately solid and chunky it is smaller than the main dwelling. The Glass House was made a National Landmark in 1997.

Johnson's Glass House 1947-1949, New Canaan, Connecticut. Image retrieved from Wikimedia Commons. Author Edelteil. [14]

The guest house on the grounds of Johnson's Glass House. Image retrieved from Wikimedia Commons. Author Staib.[15]

American architecture benefitted not only from an exchange of ideas but from the immigration of notable designers. One designer stands out about whom it can be said truly changed the face of cities with his steel and glass skyscrapers. With their simple geometry and modern construction techniques there has been no looking back and it's all due to Ludwig Mies van der Rohe.

The rise of Nazism saw the close of the Bauhaus, which Mies was director of at the time. He relocated to the United States in 1937 to head the architecture school at the Illinois Institute of Technology in Chicago. He designed the new buildings and created the overall plan for the campus. Centrally located on the campus is SR Crown Hall. Completed in 1956 Mies considered this to be his best example of a "less is more" building and in fact many consider it as his masterpiece. It is regarded as significantly important to modernist architecture and is included in the United States National Register of Historic Places.

Occupying two levels, the building is a pure rectangle and embodies industrial simplicity. The area is divided into thirds by simple planes which extend above and beyond the body of the building. Extensive use is made of glass over a steel frame. The lower two metres of glass that wraps the frame is opaque so as not to cause the occupiers to be distracted with outside occurrences whereas the top three metres has clear glass to allow light and sky views. Mies referred to the design as universal space as changes in the use of space were allowed for.

Mies' SR Crown Hall, 1950-1956 at the Illinois Institute of Technology in Chicago. Image retrieved from Wikimedia Commons. Author Joe Ravi. [16]

Mies was not the only European immigrant with design credentials. His colleague Walter Gropius, founder of the Bauhaus, also ended up in America. Both men are known for their skyscrapers constructed with plate glass curtain walls over steel girders. Curtain wall is the name for the type of construction that we see today on high rise office towers. The exterior cladding has no part to play in the structure of the building. It is secured to the steel frame.

Of course, building materials and construction techniques influenced design which was one of the foundation precepts of the International Style. The design itself should come out of the structural capability of the building materials. New materials such as reinforced steel, plate glass and reinforced concrete could be used in ways that reflected the desire for simple structures in which form and appearance could develop. This was a pillar of the new style. Finally form could be significantly simplified and with this came the industrialised mass production of materials.

Although plate glass curtain walling had been utilised as early as 1909 on the Boley Building in Kansas City, it was the Seagram Building in New York City, designed by Mies and Johnson that changed the face of modern city high rise building forever. By that time the International Style was most definitely in and decorative facades like those of the Boley Building and the 1918 Hallidie building in San Francisco were outdated. Mies was already familiar with the modern design style as some of the exterior cladding of the Bauhaus building was glass curtain walls.

The Seagram building is 157 metres tall and comprises thirty eight floors. The plate glass curtain wall is attached to the steel frame and is literally a façade, bearing no load. Its smoky grey glass seems to extend into the sky like a chimney.

Mies' Seagram Building, 1958, New York. Imaged retrieved from Wikimedia Commons. Author <u>Max Hermus</u>. [17]

Where does New Zealand architecture fit into all this? Typically we have been slow to pick up on overseas trends because of our geographical location in the world. We were about fifteen years behind the International Style and the flat-roofed simple dwellings that were constructed in New Zealand during the nineteen-thirties, although having some features of the International Style were more appropriately labelled Art Deco.

New Zealand in the 1930s saw the first Labour government and the newly established Department of Housing construction. The first State houses constructed in 1937 were virtually a blueprint for the typical New Zealand bungalow of the next thirty years. Single storey, ship-lapped weatherboard walls, detached, box-like or rectangular, tile hipped roofs and later corrugated iron roofs, and no decoration. These homes were solidly built using the very best native timber. They practically all survive today and are revered for their superior construction. The main point is that they were simple. They almost qualify as New Zealand's answer to minimalist architecture.

Later however, we took our own slant on the International Style. Designers were not keen on adopting white. They wanted to reflect the colours of the landscape, the forests. Many of the dwellings that nodded to the overseas style were constructed from timber, comprised flat roofs and an open floor plan. But far from looking proudly different they appeared modest, like a bach.

Overall modernist architecture was slow to take hold. There are examples scattered around but the government unwittingly set such a benchmark that the typical New Zealand weatherboard bungalow endured for many decades.

Throughout the 1970s to today dwellings became more complicated with multiple gables, weird shapes like a boomerang, balconies and a bathroom for every member of the family including the dog. But there has been a tendency of late to simplify design. Flat roofs are making a statement and the cube is reasserting itself. It isn't the norm, but beach communities and mountain resorts are seeing this type of architecture emerge. The designs appear more in line with 1930s Europe and United States. Perhaps New Zealand is actually eighty years behind them.

9

TINY HOUSES

"The secret of happiness, you see, is not found in seeking more, but developing the capacity to enjoy less." Socrates (469-399 BCE), Greek philosopher

Any discussion on minimalism must include tiny houses. If you absolutely had to downsize right now you would be forced to de-clutter. You could almost not afford the luxury of contemplation. You would have to be ruthless.

Who would have thought that there would be a trend away from large houses? Enormous mansions are an outward expression of wealth. As each generation successively does better than the previous one, it is a natural thing to provide the family with more bedrooms, more living areas, more bathrooms. In an age of consumerism large dwellings fit very well.

I remember growing up watching American television shows such as *The Brady Bunch* and *The Partridge Family* where large homes appeared to be the norm. I saw interesting design, spacious living areas, and even stairs inside. It was a million miles away from my reality: three bedrooms, bathroom and toilet off the hall, kitchen open to the dining room and separate lounge comprising a floor area of more or less 100 square metres. And don't even talk about individualism, style or insulation. None of that featured in architecture I was exposed to.

New Zealand soon copied what was portrayed on American television. The floor area for the average New Zealand house in 1976 was 121m².[1] By 2016 it had ballooned up to 218m². Even a standard group house, often brick veneer instead of weather board or fibrolite, comprised a large open plan living area plus a smaller formal lounge or television room. There are no walls to separate the kitchen so cooking can be more inclusive. Most homes still have a hall with access to three or four bedrooms, one with an ensuite and a giant walk-in wardrobe, bathroom, separate toilet, and the most necessary integral fully lined double garage, for these days two cars are part of the family.

This has been the norm for at least the last twenty five years – a generation. But the tide is turning with the new generation. There appear to be two reasons that the tiny house movement has gained momentum: cost of land and the building of dwellings on it is one concern and a growing awareness of the environment is another.

In many countries around the world there are cities where first home owners have little chance of owning their own home. Auckland is one such city. In 1949 the average residential property cost 2.1 times the average annual salary. Today in Auckland it is an eye-watering 8.7 times.[2]

As of 2018, the average cost in New Zealand to build the average sized dwelling is $1,800 per square metre or $392,400. [3] Building costs around the country are not uniform and in some regions it can be cheaper due to lower labour costs, or higher due to higher labour costs, difficulty of site, and geographical variation such as building on an island or being located hundreds of kilometres from a supply of construction materials. In 2017 Queenstown was the most expensive city to build a house at $3,054 per square metre and Christchurch the cheapest at $2,082 per square metre.

Mortgages aren't taken out on the cost of a building alone, rather the whole land and improvements package. Land is the secure part as far as banks are concerned, typically lending up to seventy five percent of the value. Land historically increases in value, whereas the buildings upon the land traditionally depreciate over time. But that does not mean that eventually the value of the dwelling will be reduced to zero, since the costs associated with building the house always increases. Mortgages for new builds are not subject to Reserve Bank Land Value Ratio rules, which means a borrower does not need as much deposit as if they purchased a second hand home, subject to the lender's criteria of course.

Not many entry level purchasers would build a new home these days. It's just too expensive. I'm going to run through an example of how difficult it is for an entry level purchaser to afford even a second hand house in a popular city.

Let's take the median cost of a residential property in the city of Tauranga as an example. The median house cost in Tauranga in December 2017 was $693,725.[4]Banks require a deposit of twenty percent of the property value before they will loan to a purchaser. The minimum sum required to purchase this average property therefore is $138,745, not an insignificant amount. Most first home buyers would not have this much deposit even using their compulsory retirement savings. It therefore forces them to buy in the lower price bands. However, to continue with the example, a twenty percent deposit leaves $554,980 to borrow as a mortgage. [An interesting aside – mortgage translates to "death pledge."]

To service a mortgage of $554,980 would require a minimum household income of $100,000. That's the standard 33.9 percent allowance that banks work on when calculating whether you can afford a loan. This equates to $2,812 per month or $648.92 per week. Over a typical term of thirty years the total principal of $554,980 will have been paid but also a whopping $457,340.77 of interest. And how many households would have the necessary $100,000 income? In Tauranga in 2015 the average household income was $84,000 while the national average was $91,000 [5] so there would be very few people with the ability to service a $554,980 mortgage.

Of course life gets in the way with children, redundancies or sickness so it would be difficult to maintain that level of payments throughout the course of the loan, even allowing for the natural increase in wages as one's skill level increases.

Thus, at present in New Zealand if a first home buyer can afford a property it is going to be at the bottom end of the market, a do-up, perhaps located very far away from essential services, perhaps rurally located.

Some countries such as the United Kingdom, Switzerland, Ireland and Japan operate intergenerational mortgages. The homeowner takes out a mortgage and pays interest only over the entire time he lives in the house. No principal is paid at all. Upon the death of the homeowner the mortgage debt plus the interest payments as well as the property pass to the homeowner's children. There is no fixed term on the mortgage. The beneficiary continues to repay the mortgage and still owe the capital.

It sounds horrendous to leave such a massive debt to one's children but look at it like this: the interest paid on the loan probably equates to the current market rent at the beginning of the loan. Over time instead of the "rent"/mortgage payments going up the payments remain the same. Therefore over decades the payments being made may become significantly lower than market rent.

One benefit of an intergenerational mortgage is that you get to own property and live in a neighbourhood you probably couldn't afford to under normal mortgage conditions. By paying interest only on the mortgage it's not such a squeeze on finances and it leaves a larger surplus in take home pay than if repaying principal and interest. Therefore life should be less of a struggle and much more enjoyable.

Over the course of your life that you would have been paying off a table mortgage, say twenty five to thirty years, the value of the house will have increased. It could have gone up several times its original value and at the end of that time the mortgage amount is still the same. So it's comparatively small compared to when the mortgage was originally taken out.

For the beneficiary of an intergenerational mortgage it can be useful where inheritance tax is slammed on the beneficiary. It effectively reduces the value of the property, hopefully below the inheritance tax threshold.

Of course this isn't for everyone. It's only going to work in cities where it is near impossible to get into the property market. And you can see it has special attraction to leafy suburb type localities where there is high demand for good access to particularly desirable schools, universities and job opportunities. These keep the value of property high.

New Zealand is a comparatively young country with young cities. Its population is particularly mobile and the thought of tying one's family to a city wouldn't be something many people would consider. Traditionally our high fliers test their wings overseas before returning home, if ever.

Banks are edgy about lending on apartments with tiny footprints so the owner must have a larger deposit. So there must be another way of building an affordable house.

What New Zealand and the rest of the western world is seeing is a contraction in the average dwelling size. Because the cost to own traditional residential real estate is seen as prohibitive to first home buyers an alternative is to build tiny homes. Often these are on wheels to get around Council planning laws. If fixed to the land it can be a costly exercise to obtain necessary council consents. Not that tiny houses are built with the intention of moving them. They are not caravans.

A tiny home can often be constructed out of income, meaning a mortgage does not have to be taken out. In fact, realistically a bank is unlikely to loan on a dwelling with such a small floor area even if the tiny home owner owns the land and fixes it onto foundations. Building can be completed over time as finances allow.

The land can be leased or owned. It is rare to find a vacant site unencumbered by caveats and you will never find a large subdivision where it is possible to construct a tiny house. Developers seek to get the maximum return for the sections they sell. To do this, and to entice high end purchasers they register covenants on the titles of the sections. These can range from prescribing minimum floor area for any dwelling built, prohibiting caravans on site, prohibiting the use of second hand building materials, not allowing a front fence to be constructed until a certain time frame has passed. These covenants give confidence to purchasers that the neighbourhood they are buying into will have a certain look and standard, that their property will not be devalued by the neighbour building a shack.

Therefore tiny houses are most likely to be constructed in locations on the edge of town or on small blocks of land where a land owner has cut off a block without regard for restrictive covenants. A tiny homer in this situation would more likely have a similar philosophical outlook on life and be a better fit anyway.

Tiny houses are of course cheaper to build than conventional houses. However when the laws of diminishing returns are taken into account the rate per square metre well exceeds the average construction cost across the industry. An eighteen square metre build presently costs around $63,000 or $3,500 per square metre. That doesn't include extras like a fire, gas oven and hobs, solar power, composting toilet, gas califont or double glazed windows.

Tiny homes give the occupants less space to clutter and an opportunity to carefully utilise every nook and cranny. Every purchase must be analysed since space needs to be found for it. They are perfect for the minimalist. There is absolutely no space for hoarding.

It may be that cost is the number one driver for the new tiny home movement but whether it is cost or concern for the environment, one thing is certain; there is a natural flow on effect to care for the environment. Tiny homers understand their footprint on the planet. The construction of homes twelve times smaller than the average is a huge saving in resources such as concrete foundations, framing timber, exterior cladding, interior wall and ceiling linings, window glass, fabric window coverings, and furniture. Using fewer resources equates to less energy used in extractive industries and transport which translates to less production of greenhouse gases.

It also translates to less construction waste going to landfill. It is estimated that construction and demolition waste makes up half of all waste going to landfill.[6]

Tiny homers clearly have a lighter carbon footprint. If the only repayments are to pay off the house site and not a $400,000 build as well, then the owner is less likely to feel trapped for decades putting up with a job they don't like just to pay off the mortgage.

10

VEGANISM

"Be content with what you have, rejoice in the way things are. When you realise there is nothing lacking the whole world belongs to you."
Lao Tzu, Chinese philosopher and founder of Taoism – likely 6th or 4th century BC.

When you become minimalist you begin to focus on the things in your life that are meaningful to you, what brings you joy. Clutter is eliminated. We've determined in our thought experiment that clutter causes angst. In your house there is space around treasured items. Gone are clothes you were holding onto just in case you fit them again. The chipped plates and unwanted gifts have been liberated to grace someone else's table. You overcame your emotional attachment to inanimate objects and set them free. The burden of responsibility has lifted and now you're left with only the stuff that brings you joy.

So how does veganism fit into the minimalist philosophy and which comes first? Minimalism or veganism? It really is a chicken and egg question – that's a free-ranging dirt-scratching hen and an egg laid under a hedge so no one can find it. Minimalism and veganism embrace the idea of living mindfully. That is not to say that minimalists will become vegans or vice versa. I am vegan because it is my way of protesting the mindset that animals are here to be eaten, used and abused for human gratification. Humans don't need to kill animals in order to survive.

Once upon a time in our history we did need to kill and eat animals to ensure the survival of our tribe, but those days are long gone. That was before we thought of planting fields of crops. We were hunters and gatherers. Men would cooperate to kill a bear which would feed the entire tribe and women would gather herbs and berries carrying babies in a papoose. Animals were appreciated for the sacrifice they made in order to feed humans. There was a special relationship between animals and humans that is not evident these days.

The world now produces so much food that we can choose what sort of diet we'd like to follow. The array of diets people ascribe to for health or moral reasons is astounding. And isn't it a testament to our consumerist culture that we have the choice?

There is the Paleo diet where modern humans eat the same foods as our hunter-gatherer ancestors. This consists of whole foods, lean protein, vegetables, fruit, nuts and seeds. It does not provide for grains or legumes, processed foods, sugar or dairy foods.

The Keto diet emphasizes foods low in carbohydrates and high in fat. The reduction in carbohydrates puts the body into a metabolic state called ketosis and lowers blood sugar and insulin levels.

Then there is the Calorie Restricted diet which has been popular for a few decades now. Limiting calorie intake has been shown to extend maximum lifespan. Although energy intake is reduced, the diet is high in vitamins, minerals and nutrients.

Of course the most mainstream alternative diet is vegetarian. It is an abstinence from eating meat. That's a pretty open explanation but there are many different vegetarian diets. For instance, some people do not eat red meat but will eat chicken or fish. Eating only fish is referred to as a Pescatarian diet. I cannot work this out. Presumably these people can justify the difference between mammals, birds and sea life. As far as I am aware mammals, birds and sea creatures are all living beings that reproduce. Just like us. Vegetarians also eat animal products: cheese, milk, yoghurt, honey, eggs.

Vegans, on the other hand, do not eat meat, chicken or fish, or in fact any animal that had a face or any sea creature that has feeding systems such as mussels or scallops. Vegans are mindful of all living beings. We believe that it is not our right to force another species to die in order that we may eat, or to keep another species in a manner that we would not wish to be kept in ourselves.

There was a time not so long ago that people grew their own food, including beef, lamb, chicken and pork. Now, however, with most people living in cities, few farmers grow food for many people. And now we have the rise in factory farming. It is a term we hear most often around pig or poultry production. It conjures up images of animals crammed so tightly into crates that they can't sit down or turn around. The animals suffer greatly at the hand of man. As a vegan I would say that all farming causes suffering to animals because the animals are not free to act as if they were in the wild.

These days people are removed from knowing where their food comes from, how it's produced and manipulated for consumption. The planet has thirty seven megacities,[1] or cities with populations of over ten million people. It is impractical to believe that all those inhabitants have access to farms. They would have to make a real effort to access the countryside thus it is easy to understand how we have become disconnected from the land.

In Western countries it is possible to access out of season produce year round. Countries export seasonal crops across the globe ensuring a good export price when the smaller domestic market would ordinarily see a much lower price. Whilst the exchange benefits the grower financially and consumers by satisfying demand, it can perpetuate the myth that all food is available all the time. People don't stop to think about the food growing thousands of kilometres away and being freighted by plane to their local supermarket.

Naturally, countries with the greatest populations produce the most food: China leads the world in the production of rice and pig meat, the United States in milk, chicken and beef, Brazil is one of the top five producers of milk, pork and beef and India is the second largest producer of milk and rice.[2] As you can imagine that is an awful lot of pigs and chickens to feed billions of people. Pigs are one of the most eaten animals in the world, with one billion consumed annually.[3] That's a staggering 23 million pigs per week or over three million per day, approximately 137,000 per hour and 2,300 per minute.

It's a sad indictment on the human species that we have accreditations to certify cruelty free eggs and pig products. New Zealand meat eaters can easily investigate the origins of the meat they eat. They would be shocked to learn that we import more pig products than we produce ourselves. New Zealand produces 45,000 tonnes per annum but imports 65,000 tonnes per annum predominantly from Spain with Finland, the United States and Canada making up the balance.[4] Most of the imported pig product goes to make ham, sausages and bacon. Unfortunately importing animal products means we as New Zealanders have had no say into how those animals were farmed. Many countries do not have animal welfare codes or standards.

If you live rurally or in a small town, you have a better than average chance of sourcing free range meat. Some butchers source their own free-range pigs and you can buy bacon and pork from them. If you have to eat pigs surely it is better to eat locally grown ethically produced pigs. Of course there is also the best option in my mind: don't eat meat.

Unfortunately the majority of pig-eating New Zealanders ignorantly support cruel farming practices. Animal rights, in my opinion, are slow to be enshrined in legislation but at least in this country we have some animal codes of practice that fall under the auspices of the Ministry for Primary Industries. These codes cover the treatment of all farmed animals as minimum standards. For example pig treatment is governed by the 2010 Code of Welfare for Pigs which was developed by the National Animal Advisory Committee under the Animal Welfare Act 1999. A 2015 Amendment to the Act recognises animals as sentient beings, that is, being able to experience feelings. Given that light bulb statement you would think the standards would discourage cage farming of any kind. A further amendment to the Act came into play on 1 October 2018 which provides minimum standards for poultry and pig farming as well as laying hens and meat chickens. As well as National Standards there are also animal rights groups that fight for a better life for farmed animals. Change however, comes slowly as producer boards lobby against costly animal friendly innovations.

SAFE is one organisation in New Zealand which has campaigned to ban farrowing crates where female pigs spend most of their lives, confined, cramped, giving birth to dozens of piglets, litter after litter after litter. The poor animals do not know grass, do not know how to run, do not know how to socialise. What gives us the right to do that to another species? Most people are aware of or have seen images of these beautiful animals lying on their sides with their babies suckling their teats, the mother pig stretched out unable to nuzzle her little piglets. Would we treat human mothers so inhumanely? No. So why do we do it to pigs?

We've also seen images of featherless hens crammed so tightly in cages they can't sit down. They can barely move. Captured, caged and induced to pop out eggs for uncaring barbaric humans. It's all about money: maximum eggs for minimum outlay. Farming is about making money, not making happy animals. If people saw factory farming first hand surely they'd become vegan.

If veganism or vegetarianism is not the first option for you at the very least you have a choice. Purchase free-range. Know where your food comes from. Vote for animal rights with your dollar. Animals are no less important on this planet than humans. In fact animals evolved more than five hundred million years before humans, and primates, the order to which we belong, were here some 160 million years before modern humans.

We have therefore had many millions of years to evolve into the ecological niche that we find ourselves. For humans it is as top predator. We are the single most successful species to have lived on earth, having infiltrated every continent and dominated other creatures living there. That does indeed make us sound predatory and if you applied the same scenario to crocodiles or snakes you might apply the term "ruthless killers".

In our methods of farming pigs and chickens for human consumption we are ruthless killers. It's true that New Zealand has

110

guidelines for animal care in farmed environments but it is not nearly generous enough. As a species with a very large brain we exhibit a very tiny heart. A word of warning: the following chapters will disturb.

Pig (Sus)

The domestic pig originated from the Eurasian wild boar (Sus scrofa) approximately 9,000 years ago in the Near East. The species itself is approximately five hundred thousand years old. It wasn't until the eighteenth and nineteenth centuries that Asian pigs were introduced into Europe. New Zealand has Captain James Cook to thank, or curse, for their introduction. He let pigs loose in 1769, 1773 and 1777. And didn't they love this land with no mammalian predators. They wreaked havoc on the flightless bird population. However, that is another story.

Since that time New Zealanders have hunted wild pigs in the forest. Pig dogs are specially bred to bring the pig down, tearing at its ears and head until the hunter can come and slit its throat. This is still a way of life in rural New Zealand. As distressing as this is, we can but be thankful that the wild pig had a life of its own. It's not so pretty being a pig bred for human commercial consumption.

Can you imagine spending your life in a crate unable to turn around? How would you like to feel four walls around you and concrete or steel bars beneath your feet all day and night for the three or four years that you are useful to someone else? That is the reality for most of the world's breeding pigs and approximately fifteen thousand breeding sows in New Zealand per annum.[5] The sow is put into a crate five days before giving birth until the piglets are weaned, four weeks later. These little piglets have short lives, being slaughtered for bacon at four to seven months and for pork before the age of six months.

Sows are viewed as nothing more than baby factories turning out piglets for human consumption. Their lives are cut short by their inability to sustain the rate of production demanded of them and they are slaughtered at three to five years. A pig's natural lifespan is ten to twelve years.

In New Zealand ninety percent of pig products come from factories.[8] This is where female pigs are cast in tiny boxes to give birth. These are called farrowing crates. They imprison the sow who cannot turn around to even nuzzle her own piglets. She can stand and lie down. That's it. Let me put that another way: She can't even turn around. There is no straw, no organic material in which to nestle, or smell or delight in. No organic natural system is used to absorb her waste. There is nothing natural or thoughtful about the environment in which a factory farmed sow spends her life. A naturally social intelligent being lies listless, lethargic and depressed, reduced to being a baby factory, impregnated continually until four years of age. She exhibits classic distressed behaviour such as licking the bars or rubbing against them. The environment makes her sick. Then she is shipped off to the abattoir to be slaughtered for food. These beautiful animals finally see a glimpse of sun, experience fresh air for the first time in their lives and then all too quickly experience fear again as they smell blood and hear the squeals of the animals ahead of them.

Farmers defend this practice as necessary to prevent the sow rolling over and crushing her piglets. Why not then let them breed naturally in large roomy nesting stalls in paddocks where they are free to exhibit normal nurturing behaviour?

The farrowing crate environment is stressful not only for the mother, but also for the piglets. They exhibit stress-related behaviour such as cannibalism. But the farmer has an answer to that. He cuts off their tails and with pliers nips off the ends of their teeth. And don't imagine for one minute that this is done with anaesthetic. The male piglets are castrated similarly. At only four weeks old the piglets are taken from their mother.

SAFE (Save Animals from Experiments) delivered to Parliament a 110,000 signature petition on 15 March 2018 to get sow crates outlawed. SAFE estimate there are 28,800 breeding sows in the country at any given time. Fifteen thousand will be trapped in these tiny metal cages, bare of any straw, housed in windowless factories, impregnated to produce 2.5 litters per year.[9]

Unbelievably these crates are approved by the National Animal Welfare Advisory Committee who states the crates are better for the piglets and sows believing if the sows were not so confined they would squash their piglets to death. I shake my head. They only have to put themselves in the same situation as the pigs to know that this is cruel and wrong.

Thankfully not all farms are like this. Freedom Farms and the SPCA operate free-range farms for pork production. Pigs are free to roam in grass paddocks. The sows use farrowing huts which comprise a deep bed of straw in an open A-frame shelter. The waste straw is later composted and thus recycled. The mother is able to naturally nurture her piglets, the most natural thing in the world.

Slaughter Ages		
	Slaughtered	Natural life
Pigs – breeding sows	3-5 years	10-12 years
Pigs – bacon	4-7 months	
Pigs – pork	up to 6 months	
Lambs	6-8 months	12-14 years
Beef	18 months	15-20 years
	4 years	15-20 years

[Source: Vegetarian Society]

Pigs are spectacularly intelligent animals. Lori Marino and Christina Colvin from Emory University, Atlanta released a study in 2015 which was published by the Nonhuman Rights Project. They reviewed multiple studies on pigs and other animals. Their conclusions on pigs are remarkable. Here are some of their findings.

Pigs have excellent long term memories. They can negotiate mazes and other locating object tests, they learn from each other in groups, can understand simple symbolic language, they can learn combinations of symbols for actions and objects, play with each other, co-operate with one another, can manipulate a joy stick to move an on-screen cursor and exhibit empathy. They outperform three year old children in cognition tests and animal experts consider them more trainable than cats and dogs. Pigs dream and see in colour. They can be picky eaters. They are hygienic, not defecating near their living space. Pigs are sociable. They like to cuddle and snuggle nose to nose when sleeping and who doesn't like to do that? In the wild they live in matriarchal societies. PETA (People for the Ethical Treatment of Animals) notes they are naturally slender. It is we who over feed them. Considering all these wonderful attributes is it any wonder George Orwell chose Major the pig to be the top animal in the farmyard?

Pigs are so clever that ranked in intelligence they are right up there behind chimps and more or less equal with dolphins.[10]It is fair to say that this is a representative ranking because there are dozens of animal rankings for intelligence. However, most of those listed below feature on most lists, whatever the order. The ranking below has pigs as the second most intelligent on the planet. Why then, are pigs so maligned and treated so cruelly without dignity?

The top ten most intelligent animals

1. Chimps

2. Pigs

3. Dolphins

4. Parrots

5. Whales

6. Dogs

7. Octopus

8. Elephants

9. Squirrels

10. Cats

[App.com Part of USA Today Network, 17/7/16]

We have companion animals such as cats and dogs and yet pigs far outperform them as intelligent, playful and social beings. In the west we don't eat our cats and dogs and we find it repugnant to be exposed to such practices when we travel. We also find it abhorrent to use cats and dogs in experimental research, science or teaching. Therefore, the pig is the animal of choice for experimental science. What is the pig's crime for such cruel treatment? Perhaps only the fact that humans have not formed an emotional attachment to them in the same way that we have with cats and dogs. However, biological evolution also played a hand.

Pigs are omnivores and their physiology is remarkably similar to ours. Pig organ systems are 80-90% similar to corresponding systems in humans. These similarities make them, in research terms, translational models. Therefore if something works on a pig it's probably going to work on a human.

For more than thirty years pigs have been used in medical procedures. Pig bladder tissues have been used to re-grow human leg muscles. Defective human heart valves have been replaced with tissues derived from pig hearts which can deliver an additional fifteen years of life for the recipient.[7]

It seems there is no shortage of research ideas as pigs continue to be used for renal research and dermatological, toxicology, pharmacology and transplantation studies. The USA National Institutes of Health announced in April 2014 the successful transplant of hearts from genetically engineered pigs into baboons, with an eye to replicating this on humans in the future [11].

Research is presently underway to develop pig lungs that could be compatible with the human body. This necessitates editing the pig genome and as human transplantation organ supply is never met, these developments are vital research for medicine. This 'usefulness' of pigs to the human race is what appears to have sealed their fate.

Chickens

Gallus gallusdomesticus

The humble and delightful chicken that we know today was domesticated in South East Asia approximately 8,000 years ago from the Red Jungle Fowl. The chicken is such a favourite that we have the New Zealand Poultry, Pigeon & Bird Association which shows many varieties of fowl and other cage birds.

It's hard to reconcile the image of washed and blow dried chickens lovingly paraded at A & P shows, the subject of the hilarious Pecking Order movie, with the small frozen packages in the deep freeze of the supermarket. And to be fair most people wouldn't link the two. We seem to be incredibly skilled at projecting human qualities onto cartoon animals such as the gorgeous barnyard characters in Chicken Run, and then totally shutting off our emotions to tuck into a lovely chicken casserole. I bet some people have watched Pecking Order and Chicken Run whilst eating chicken and not even made the connection.

So how then do poultry fare in the humane treatment stakes? Obviously if it was all fluffy bunnies for these beautiful birds there would not be standards and guidelines, or codes of ethics, nor an overarching Ministry. In 2015 New Zealanders consumed 20 chickens per person.[10] The growth in consumption is approximately six percent per annum.[11] Therefore by my calculations, in 2018 New Zealanders could have consumed as much as twenty four chickens each. The majority of these birds are not grown as free range but in densely populated barns. Meat chickens are not caged.

Here is an interesting fact about meat chickens: They are not the same breed as hen laying chickens. Hen layers don't have the right body structure to supply meat. New Zealand meat chickens are typically Cobb, developed by the venture capital company, Cobb Vantress and the Ross, developed by Aviagen in Scotland. Globally more than 55 million chickens are eaten every single day and they are all female. There is no place in the poultry industry for male chickens. Within hours of hatching they are electrocuted, gassed or ground up alive.

Meat chickens, called broilers in the poultry industry, are bred for rapid weight gain. Eggs are placed in incubators until they hatch at twenty one days. At one day old they are transported to the rearing farm where they travel along a conveyor belt and are dropped into modules. They are sprayed with vaccines against disease as they go. Their environment for the five to seven weeks that they are alive is inside a noisy, smelly shed which has automated feed systems, twenty-four hour a day artificial lighting and no access to the outside. The litter on the floor is only replaced between new batches of birds. These sheds can house up to twenty thousand chickens and under New Zealand's Code of Welfare for meat chickens the stocking rate must be less than thirty chickens per square metre.[12] If this disturbs you and convinces you to switch to free range chickens, be aware that even free range chickens are more often than not barn bred. They simply have access to outdoors. You need to ask some questions of your retailer to determine the provenance of your meat chicken.

Perhaps because meat chickens are not bred in cages their plight does not elicit the same emotive response as hen laying chickens. Incidentally, a female chicken is called a pullet until she lays her first egg and then she is a hen. That's at about sixteen to twenty weeks in the industry. By thirty five weeks old she's at the peak of her production.

New Zealand layer hens are likely to be Hyline Brown or Brown Shavers. They lay an egg a day until they are about eight months old. That's quite different to their Red Jungle Fowl ancestor which lays one to two clutches per year at four to six eggs each time. The exhaustive production of eggs has an effect on the chickens who must consume calcium in order to produce an eggshell. Intensely farmed chickens do not grow strong bones as calcium and phosphorus is drawn from the body's natural reserves and transferred to the shell of the egg.

At present there are four methods of housing laying hens. We have all seen images of the achingly sad life of a cage chicken. We've all seen images of birds crammed into metal cages, stressed and upset. These cages are being phased out by the end of 2022. The Ministry of Primary Industries Code of Welfare for layer hens, 1 October 2018, makes it illegal to keep birds in such conditions.

The new cages come under Minimum Standard 4 – Housing and Equipment Design Construction and Maintenance. Cages should adhere to the following regulations:

i.   Multi deck cages are to be arranged so the hens below are not defecated on;

ii.   Manure must be removed from under a cage before it accumulates to touch the cage floor;

iii. All cages for layer hens must have a floor slope not exceeding eight degrees which supports forward facing claws;

- A cage height of at least forty centimetres over sixty five percent of the cage floor area and not less than thirty five centimetres at any point;

- Access for each hen to at least two drinking points;

- Suitable claw shortening devices fitted if modifications are made to cages.

<u>Colony Cages</u> As the name suggests there are a number of birds in a colony. There can be up to sixty birds and the minimum area per bird allowed is seven hundred and fifty square centimetres. That isn't a lot but at least the bird can sit down, turn around and ruffle her feathers. A colony cage provides nest boxes, perches and scratch pads. Food and water is always available and as with conventional cages a conveyor belt below the cage removes faecal matter. They do not have access to fresh air and sunshine.

<u>Barn</u> These eggs are commonly marketed as "cage free". Only three percent of New Zealand farms raise barn eggs.[13] These huge sheds can house as many as five thousand hens with the stocking rate being seven hens per square metre. There is litter on the floor, as well as perches and nest boxes. The birds have no access to the outside.

<u>Free Range</u> As with barn but the hens have access to the outside.

The best and surest option of purchasing true free range eggs is to buy from a friend or farmers markets. People are passionate about the eggs they sell. They love their chooks and they love that people want to do the right thing by the hens.

SPCA Blue Tick Farms and The Five Freedoms

The SPCA Blue Tick farmers operate their farms under the philosophy of the Five Freedoms. It's pretty simple actually and as you read through them I invite you to apply these freedoms to yourself and your family. The SPCA Blue Tick farms are guided by these principles, which are generic, I think, to a world which we share with animals.

i. Freedom from thirst, hunger and malnutrition. Animals must have access to fresh food and water and must not be kept in such an environment that they need to compete for food.

ii. Freedom from discomfort. Animals should have appropriate shelter, resting and weatherproof areas.

iii. Freedom from pain, injury and disease. Producers are to supply health plans in consultation with veterinarians.

iv. Freedom to express natural and normal behaviour appropriate to the animal's age. This ensures they are provided with the space, facilities and the company of other animals.

v. Freedom from fear and distress. Conditions and treatment of the animals must be such to avoid mental suffering.

As the top predator I believe it is incumbent on us to treat animals with compassion and dignity. It is pure luck that we have large brains and many skills to ensure we don't go hungry. Imagine a world where we exerted kindness and compassion with equal amounts of brain power. How different that world would be. Becoming vegan is to exercise compassion and empathy.

Cows

Bos Taurus

Raising dairy cows for human milk consumption has a detrimental effect on the planet. It is a huge cost to the environment. In New Zealand there has been a surge in the production of milk. This is because we compete for export earnings by volume of milk produced. Little New Zealand is out there competing with the likes of China, United States, India and Brazil which are major suppliers of the world's milk.[15] New Zealand could be adding value to milk instead of competing with countries that can outstrip our production on a like for like basis. We could, for example, farm milk organically and certify it as such. It would attract a premium price and we would not need to produce the enormous volume of milk powder that we do. But while milk is touted by the dairy industry as white gold little is going to change.

In the years 2008-2014 New Zealand milk production more than doubled from 677,000 tonnes to 1,460,000 tonnes, with China sales accounting for the extra production. Over the same period Chinese production for its

own milk increased fifteen fold.[16] New Zealand milk powder production peaked in 2014 but dropped back in 2016 to 1,370,000 tonnes.[16]

Dairy farms are two and three times the size they were fifty years ago. Fabulous global milk powder prices pushed up demand for land and for conversion to dairy farms on areas previously unknown for dairy production such as Southland and the West Coast of the South Island. Today dairy farms occupy 1.7 million hectares[16] and as of December 2017, 6.5 million milking cows[17] in 11,748 herds. The 2016/2017 season produced 21 billion litres of milk earning export revenue of $NZ13.4 billion. [16]

Obviously with this level of revenue the dairy industry is very important to New Zealand. Multi-million dollar milking sheds put through four hundred plus cows once or twice a day, depending on the time of year. Grass doesn't grow at a constant rate throughout the year but the cows have to eat. The farmer has massive loans against his farm to fund the rotary cowshed and the tractors. He can't afford not to milk cows so he installs a great big silo, or two or three of them and fills it full of palm kernels as supplementary feed. Yes, you did read that right. Palm kernel. We will explore that in chapter eleven.

Dairy farmers traditionally bale silage for the herd's winter feed. The grass for this is grown during times of plenty in the spring and summer, usually on farm, but often on the farmer's run-off, a supplementary block of land that is away from the main farm and offers a different growing environment. But the fact that it is now common practice to import palm kernel implies that the land itself cannot support the huge numbers of cows. The farmer is trapped by needing to pay off debt so is reluctant to reduce the herd number to a sustainable amount. If a farmer is buying in feed then that farm is not sustainable.

There has been much talk of palm oil and palm kernel recently but I don't believe enough of us understand how detrimental the growing of the stuff is. After all, we don't grow it in New Zealand so we don't see the harm to the environment first hand.

Virgin rainforest in Asia is razed to the ground, threatening to extinction animals that call it home. The cleared land is planted with a single crop – palm. The resulting oil and kernels are ubiquitous. You just can't get away from the stuff. Read the labels of your supermarket shopping very carefully. Today I found a new product on the shelf. Locally made biscuits beautifully packaged and marketed as dairy free, egg free and gluten free. My heart soared. I read the ingredients list and there it was. Palm. I was shocked because I thought this company understood. I thought they'd got it. They're doing all the right things for hens and dairy cows, but not for orangutans and the rainforest. It proves to me that this company isn't at all interested in ethics.

I digress. The problems with palm are so disturbing it is covered later in the book under Environmentalism. Let's get back to the cows.

The palm kernel to feed cows in 2017 was slightly less than two million tonnes at a cost of $264 per tonne. It is shipped thousands of kilometres to New Zealand which transportation produces nasty greenhouse gases and thus contribute to the warming of our planet. The kernels are fed to cows on overstocked farms. How is that even economical? Unfortunately it is because palm plantations are being planted so fast that the price for the stuff is ridiculously cheap and if the normal laws of economics apply, it will get cheaper as the stuff floods the market.

So much is being asked of the land that it has to be continually dosed with fertiliser. In fact the amount of grass that is grown today would not have been possible before 1913 with the commercialisation of the Haber-Bosch process to convert atmospheric nitrogen into ammonium. Suddenly something other than clover was available to help grass grow better. One hundred years on dairy land is crucially dependent on a fertiliser regime.

Fertiliser is a magic bullet. It has a critical part to play in feeding the world's 7.2 billion people. Without it the earth would only be able to support 4 billion people.[18] Up until 1913, that is, in the ten thousand years that we've been growing crops and farming animals, if we wanted to grow more food we simply tilled more land. The Haber-Bosch process completely changed this. Nitrogen in the air is triple bonded to other nitrogen atoms but the nitrogen needs to bond with hydrogen to form ammonia. The Haber-Bosch process uses a lot of fossil fuel energy to accomplish this. Presently the world produces 186 million tonnes of fertiliser annually comprising nitrogen, phosphate and potash.[19] One percent of the entire world's energy supply is consumed to produce it.[20] This of course contributes to the release of carbon into the atmosphere.

Most nitrogen ends up in water or the air as nitrous oxide. It pollutes drinking water, creates acid rain, acidic soil and threatens ecosystems. An excess of nitrogen in water creates algal blooms which block light to the water column, resulting in the deaths of fish.

Despite the environmental effects of fertiliser use, its demand is expected to double in the next one hundred years.[21] Therefore we can expect more marginal land to be brought into production.

Of course we also have all that methane farting into the atmosphere. Cows produce between 70 and 120 kilograms of methane annually.[22] In New Zealand half our greenhouse gas emissions are from methane and agriculture. This topic is so important it is discussed in the Environmental chapter.

It's not just nitrogen fertiliser and methane that is cause for concern. There is the one thousand litres of water that it takes to produce one litre of milk. Say that again. One thousand litres of water? To make one litre of milk? How can it be that much? Well first the grass has to grow. It doesn't grow in a desert. A cow drinks between 11 and 113 litres of water per day depending on which part of her life cycle she is at. Then there is the high pressure hosing down of the concrete yards around the milking shed, typically twice per day. The milk is then transported off farm to the factory where it is processed before being packaged and sent to market.

Incidentally, growing beef is actually much more resource intensive. It takes a staggering fifteen thousand litres of water to produce one kilogram of beef. Pork and bacon come off a little better at six thousand litres. Butter takes almost as much at five and a half thousand litres of water to produce one kilogram. Eggs come in at around three thousand litres. Compare this to vegetables which require an average three hundred and twenty two litres of water to grow one kilogram of vegetables.

Meanwhile Daisy, AKA number 790, is assessed for each litre of milk she produces and when her rate drops that's the end of her. She's walked thousands of kilometres over her lifetime, back and forth to the milking shed, calved every year and been allowed to be with her calf less than four days each year. She's stood in treeless paddocks during blazing droughts and huddled with her kind on frosty or snowy days when the grass wasn't available, trapped frustratingly beneath the ice. She's endured the indignity of having a mechanical suction cup stuck to her teats while being blasted with the farmer's awful choice of music. She's possibly suffered verbal or physical abuse at the hands of impatient or cruel farm workers. She has been forced into slave labour just so that a human can drink her milk. You'd think she could spend her unproductive days happily eating grass. But no. She's trucked off to the works and slaughtered for pet food.

Where is the compassion for living beings? We show compassion to other humans; the old and the sick, the young and the misfits. We don't kill the weak or abandon them like most other species do. We do exhibit compassion but it is not across all species.

Litres of water used in the production of 1 kg of food

Chocolate	17,196
Beef	15,415
Sheep meat	10,412
Pork	6,000
Butter	5,553
Bacon	6,000
Chicken meat	4,325
Cheese	3,178
Eggs	3,000
Rice	2,497
Bread	1,608
Milk	1,000
Apples	822
Bananas	790
Potatoes	287
Wine (250mls)	109
Beer (250mls)	74
Tea (250mls)	27

[Institute Mechanical Engineers]

Eating for the Environment

Vegans traditionally have animal suffering in mind when reasoning their diet choice. However, there is a movement afoot that proposes veganism as an option to save the planet. Minimalists, in focusing on mindful living, can extend their practice to mindful eating. And this is where a minimalist's journey towards veganism begins. As minimal consumers we have the chance to really think about the origin of our food. And if you want to be lighter on the planet, then consuming a plant based diet is the only way to go. The current world population is 7.2 billion. The planet cannot support billions of meat eaters.

Extinction

Not all vegans are driven by a love of animals in their diet choice. Some identify with the sustainability of the environment that the diet promotes. The world is a diverse place. There are around ten thousand bird species which has been revised upwards to eighteen thousand species based on major new studies,[23] five and a half million insect species, up to two million animal species, and one million aquatic species. It seems perverse that the species I belong to, one of the smallest groups, seems intent on obliterating every other species off the face of the planet.

On Earth there are only five billion hectares of agricultural land.[24] Considering what we know about the other planets in our solar system we can extend this statement to: in our galaxy there are only five billion hectares of agricultural land. It seems a crazy concept but I want to emphasize how incredibly precious land is. A staggering sixty eight percent of that land is dedicated to raising livestock. That's about 3.4 billion hectares, or less than half a hectare for every person on earth. This one factor is a large contributor to greenhouse gas emissions. It is estimated that between a quarter and a third of all man-made greenhouse emissions come from food production and that the bulk of this comes from farming animals.

You may think you are too small or unimportant to be an affecter of change. But consider this: in the Western world a family of four meat eaters emits more greenhouse gases than driving two cars. When we drive cars we can, if we choose to, think about the petrol we use for fuel. We can think about the release of carbon dioxide and methane (also a carbon molecule) into the atmosphere as we burn that fuel. But it is much harder to equate eating meat with the release of greenhouse gases. We need to bring this in closer, to relate it to something we are familiar with.

Imagine your typical quarter pounder hamburger. Eating that hamburger is the equivalent of driving your car 6.3 kilometres. Now go to your potato cupboard and measure out a quarter pound of potatoes, that's 113 grams. Growing those spuds emitted the greenhouse gas equivalent of driving your car a mere 100 metres.

The Oxford Martin School Future Food Programme in Oxford University estimates that if everyone in the world changed to a plant based diet by the year 2050, then greenhouse emissions would decline by seventy percent.

The United Nations puts the current global population at seven billion two hundred thousand. By 2030 there will be 8.6 billion. By 2050 it is projected there will be 9.8 billion people and by 2100 the human species will top 11.2 billion individuals. We can't all be eating meat. Something is going to have to change. The planet will not support 11 billion meat eaters. An interesting aside: the planet presently produces enough food to support 12 billion people but due to economics, wars, natural disaster, political instability and the fact that approximately one third of food produced is discarded, nearly eight million people meet a daily challenge to access food.[25]

Hunting and gathering societies were human's first and most successful adaptation. In fact this type of society existed for ninety percent of human history. These people were constantly on the move and therefore they could not carry much. They were the ultimate minimalists. They didn't own property, not even livestock. In contrast to today's minimalists however, rather than contemplate the joy that the freedom of the burden of ownership gave them, their thoughts and time were devoted to getting enough to eat.

In this respect we were no different to other primates. Life was lived in the present. There was no preserving or pickling fruit for the future. If a homo sapien happened upon a lion's kill he might have been lucky enough to scare it away or kill it in order to share in a bit of meat. Or at worst, after the lions, hyenas and vultures had their fill, suck the marrow from the bones which most animals aren't able to do.

But real hunting required a cognitive leap in our development. It required the co-operation of large numbers of homo sapiens and this didn't happen for many more years. Only ten thousand years ago with the spread of Neolithic man did homo sapiens band together to make a kill. Later there was a change to agriculture. The saving and planting of seed meant humans needed to settle near the crops. This was a dramatic change in the way we lived. It meant we could stay in one place and more or less safely raise a family. As long as the family and the wider village tended to the needs of the farm then no one should go hungry. That's the theory.

But crop growing has its own demands. Single crop agriculture is susceptible to soil erosion. When forest or other land cover is stripped away for the replanting of a single crop the topsoil is exposed to sun, wind and rain in a way that it wasn't previously. Rain, instead of filtering down through a canopy of leaves and branches to percolate gently into the soil, hits the soil with whole raindrops. These pick up micro particles of soil and run off the newly planted land moving the soil from one place to another before either soaking into the soil or evaporating. Mono-crop agriculture therefore increases evaporation rates as more soil is exposed to the sun.

Disease is a risk with mono-crop agriculture. Specialty insects or bacteria find a whole plantation of their desired food and no natural check on their numbers. So when they get their foot in the door the only course open to the grower is to use insecticides. Don't the insects sound like the actions of humans? Remember the bison migrations across the North American plains, or the New Zealand orange roughy fishery? It was so exciting for the human species to discover a new food resource, that pretty soon the resource was depleted to near extinction.

These new crops required water so the humans had to divert rivers. But diverting rivers creates flooding, an unforeseen and unfortunate consequence in pre-modern times. Crops are subject to the vagaries of the seasons and all the weather extremes that come with that. Now, people were tied to the land in a way that they never had been before.

With this tie came the domestication of animals not only for eating but for transport and ploughing. Suddenly we owned things: agricultural equipment, things to put in houses. We had centralised government, political structures, trade, specialisation and the division of labour.

The division of labour. Great tomes have been written on this subject. Here I mean to point out that with the co-operation of people to grow food and to trade it, came concepts of owners and workers or overseers and slaves. There are many steps in the supply chain of getting produce to the table from saving the seed, planting it, tending the crop, harvesting the produce, preserving it, cooking it. Through the many hands the product passes, the workers do not share equally in its rewards of production. Contrast this with subsistence farming where one family would have carried out the entire process for themselves.   The same goes for raising animals for food. As soon as someone gets into the business of farming animals for trade they get into supply chains and economies of scale. This inevitably is not good news for the animals.

Let's jump forward ten thousand years. In Henry David Thoreau's 1854 treatise "On Higher Laws" he ponders this norm of eating animals. He discusses whether hunting wild animals and eating meat is necessary. He concludes that the primitive, carnal sensuality of humans drive them to kill and eat animals, and that a person who transcends this propensity is superior to those who cannot. The highest form of self-restraint is when one can subsist not on other animals, but rather on plants and crops cultivated from the earth.

It's a phrase worth contemplating and repeating. *The highest form of self-restraint is when one can subsist not on other animals, but on plants and crops cultivated from the earth.* It is clear that Thoreau considered himself as an animal. He viewed humans as a family in the order of primates.

I suspect that Thoreau did not foresee a time when the planet would have to feed nine billion people. If he had he would have been astute enough to know that so many humans could not be sustained by such unethical practices as eating animals.

There is no doubt that veganism frees one from guilt and it propels the practitioner to engage in ethical practices in other aspects of their life. Contemplate the chart below. Interesting that humans are the most recently evolved species and yet have no compunction whatsoever in eating all the other groups.

Age of Species on Earth

Land plants	443 million years
Fish	417 million years
Reptiles	290 million years
Primitive mammals	248 million years
Flowering plants	142 million years
Birds	60 million years
Modern mammals	33.7 million years
Insects	5.5 million years
Beetles	1.5 million years
Aquatic	1 million years
Humans	300,000 years

Thornton, Jocelyn, The Reed Field Guide to New Zealand Geology. An introduction to rocks, minerals and fossils, Reed, 1985

Gibbs, George, Ghosts of Gondwana, The History of Life in New Zealand, Craig Potton, 2007

Nutrition

It is a common misconception that people following a vegan diet miss out on essential vitamins and minerals. Everything we need is readily available from a plant-based diet. The trick is to be very well informed before you change your lifestyle for the better. Before I became vegan I researched my daily requirements of essential elements; calcium, protein, vitamin B12. I was paranoid about getting my daily requirements for a woman of my age. I put on weight! Now I don't put on weight easily and I had to get to the bottom of that. I found I was eating more than I wanted to. Then I did the maths. I was dutifully almost obtaining my daily minimum requirements in the crucial categories but when I compared those figures to those of my previous diet, I quickly realised that actually, I'd probably never met my supposed recommended daily intake in my life. I am a small eater and I know what and how much I should be eating. It was a great lesson. For the first few months I was protein counting and it set me up for life. I got into good habits and now I instinctively know what is going to give me the biggest bang for my buck. I eat purposefully and mindfully. I eat to make it count. I don't bulk up on something that isn't going to benefit my overall nutrition plan. That doesn't mean to say I don't eat French fries now and again. I'm only human.

I think the biggest challenge for people in converting to a plant-based diet is the concept of substitution. It's hard to get your head around going from meat and three veg to a nut roast. Don't do that. Don't think substitution. Vegan food is so much more interesting and adventurous. For example, how yummy is Mexican chilli beans and corn chips? You don't want to spoil that with cheese and sour cream but you can add super thick sour Greek coconut yogurt. Many cultures around the world are dairy-free and meat free. When you take the plunge to eat only a plant-based diet you invite the rest of the world into your kitchen. As least that's what happened with me.

It's helpful to have an idea of what your food provides before you simply cut out animal products. That way you can be sure of eating to make it count as opposed to eating just to fill a hole.

There are seven essential elements to a healthy diet: carbohydrates, proteins, fats, minerals, vitamins, fibre and water.

Carbohydrates provide energy so you're going to need brown rice, bread and pasta. I stay away from white rice. It doesn't benefit me in the slightest. I can't believe Indian restaurants only serve white rice. And pulse pasta is a brilliant option for adding protein to a meal, something wheat pasta doesn't do.

Of course protein is the biggie for vegans. The single most asked question to vegans is "Where do you get your protein from?" Necessary for the body's growth and repair, protein is found in pulses and legumes, nuts, peas, lentils and beans in worthwhile amounts. And it's scattered around in a host of other foods. Reading labels is your best educator so take your glasses to the supermarket.

Minerals and vitamins maintain health. You only have to think of old time sailors and the scurvy problem to realise how important fresh fruit and vegetables are. Vegetables are naturally low in fat and calories and do not contain cholesterol. Vegan diets are high in fresh produce which provide us with potassium, phosphorus, magnesium and vitamins A, C and E. Mushrooms are a special wonder food. As well as providing vitamin D, which they continue to absorb if you place them on your window sill, they are one of the few foods available to vegans to provide vitamin B12. This vitamin is necessary for protecting nerves and red blood cells, and preventing anaemia. It comes from micro-organisms and is found in all animal derived food but for vegans it is obtained from mushrooms, seaweed, soy (tofu/tempeh), yeast and yeast extract (marmite). There are breads fortified with B12. It's a case of reading labels. If you are not sure about the amount of B12 you are obtaining you can use a plant-based supplement.

Vitamin D strengthens bones and teeth. It is absorbed into our bodies from sunlight. Rest home residents take supplementary vitamin D because they typically do not go outside.

Calcium is crucial for bone health. Sources are leafy greens, nuts, soy, fruit and vegetables, grains, beans and dried fruit.

Omega 3 is a fatty acid important for maintaining healthy hearts, eye and brain function. It is obtained from ground flaxseed, walnuts, canola oil, soy.

Iron is necessary for absorbing oxygen into the bloodstream and transporting it to the cells. It is available in dark chocolate, cocoa powder, tofu, grains, beans, pulses, nuts, pumpkin seeds, sundried tomatoes, dried apricots, parsley, spinach, dried coconut, olives, currants, raisins, lentil sprouts.

Fibre is important in keeping food moving through the gut. A word of warning about shop bought cereals. They are loaded with sugar. You might typically find twenty grams of sugar in a one hundred gram serving. Read the boxes. It takes less than half an hour for me to make my own toasted muesli. Here is the recipe:

Bake three cups of rolled oats for fifteen minutes at 160 ° C. Add one cup of chopped nuts, one cup of coconut and a heaped tablespoon each of sesame seeds, ground flaxseed and ground almonds. Roast a further ten minutes. When cool add one cup of mixed dried fruit and a sprinkle of pumpkin seeds, whole almonds and flaked coconut. Store and enjoy for brekkie with coconut yoghurt, stewed fruit and almond milk.

An interesting side effect of a plant-based diet is that you break the sugar addiction. Because you aren't in the substitution game, you're not trying to create plant based banana cakes loaded with sugar and oil and sweet frosting. Far easier to throw into a blender dates, oats, nuts, dried fruit and cocoa to make Bliss balls. The dates hold everything together, the fruit sweetens it. I even throw in dark chocolate which is dairy-free. Sometimes I strike unblended chunks. What a treat.

Breaking the sugar addiction was the most surprising and delightful consequence of becoming vegan. I couldn't care less about desserts now. Not interested. That is a shocking departure from the old me, who couldn't wait to finish my main so I could get to dessert.

No discussion on veganism would be complete without comparing meats to nuts. In New Zealand we are world renowned for the quality of the lamb and beef that we produce. Lamb and beef boards were established a hundred years ago to serve the interests of the farmer producers. Winning Olympian athletes are used in advertising to extol enormous benefits of eating meat. They disingenuously compare, for example, a beef steak or a lamb chop to an enormous plate of spinach. The inference is obvious. What they should be comparing to meat are nuts.

Nuts provide an extraordinary array of beneficial goodies including calcium, protein, dietary fibre, folate, vitamin E, magnesium, copper and potassium as well as healthy mono and poly-unsaturated fatty acids. The traditional Mediterranean diet is high in nuts as is the traditional Nordic diet. Both regions have historically longer life expectancies than other regions. A United States study found that people with the highest nut intakes had a thirty-four percent lower risk of heart disease. This is backed up by a European study of 400,000 participants where twenty-nine percent had a lower risk and a Spanish study of 7,500 people which showed a thirty percent reduction in cardiovascular events.[26]

So, can you eat too many nuts? Of course. Over-eating anything is not good. Generally, nuts are high in calories, but each nut type has beneficial vitamins. You want to make sure these stay at healthy levels rather than spike due to eating too many nuts.

You should aim to eat approximately twenty eight grams per day which equates to one serving of the following:

23 almonds, or

5 cashews, or

7 walnuts, or

1-2 handfuls of pistachios, or

15 pecan halves, or

2 Brazil nuts, or

1 handful of hazelnuts.

One argument in favour of eating meat is that we've done it forever. And in the interests of a balanced argument, let's take a look at what beef can provide our bodies. It is primarily composed of protein and fat. One hundred grams of beef contains:

Calories	217
Water	61%
Protein	26.1 grams
Carbohydrates	0
Sugar	0
Fibre	0
Fat	11.8 grams

Beef also contains B12, essential for blood formation and maintaining the brain and nervous system, higher amounts of iron than chicken or fish and selenium, niacin (B3), zinc and phosphorus. The protein contains all nine amino acids which are required for growth and maintenance of the body.

Our ancestors were hunter gatherers and our teeth and digestive systems have adapted accordingly. Our large brains require a lot of protein to function and eating animals provides this. However, we are not the only large animals on the planet. Elephants, giraffes, wildebeest: all formidable animals that survive on plant diets. Our primate cousins, lemurs and apes, never moved away from eating plants, although chimps have been observed eating one of their own after a fight.

Health

Humans are omnivores. This is an indisputable fact. Our physiology determines that we have evolved to eat plants and animals. Our teeth have features of both herbivores and carnivores. Plant eating animals have wide flat molars for grinding foliage. They also chew in a horizontal motion which is typical for grinding. Of course we too have wide flat molars.

Carnivores have sharp, narrow incisors to rip meat off bones and they chew in a vertical manner. Observe your cat or dog and notice how different the mouth action is compared to a horse. But it is the same action as us.

The digestive tracts of herbivores, carnivores and omnivores differ in length and, as you might expect, omnivore digestive tract lengths lie somewhere in between herbivores and carnivores. Herbivores have the longest tract, up to twenty seven times longer than the length of the animal.[27] This is because plants consist of cellulose which is a particularly large molecule and difficult to digest. The digestive tract contains billions upon billions of bacteria to break down the food. Meat, on the other hand, is easily broken down and not so many billions of bacteria are required.

The gut has two types of digestive juices which break down food; alkaloids specialise in breaking down whole grains, bread, fruit and vegetables, whereas hydrochloric acid works on meat. But acids need help in the form of the calcium that is readily available in the body. It sucks the calcium away from bones and puts it to work breaking down meat in the gut. Unfortunately the body does not replace the calcium as fast as it is utilised and the net result is that meat eaters have less bone density than non-meat eaters.[28]

Why would some animals evolve to eat meat and others evolve to eat plants? Some of the planet's largest animals eat only plants. Even the dinosaurs ate exclusively plants. Other great vegan animals are elephants, rhinoceros, hippopotamus, bison, wildebeest, horses, manatees, deer and yaks. Gorillas principally consume foliage but have a taste for termites and ants and will destroy their nests to access them, so we can't count them.

The answer to the question is simply food supply. Most of evolution is a response to securing available food. If you visualise the animals above, they are surrounded by food and if, in the case of grasslands in Africa, the grass withers, the animals migrate to greener pastures. Only where there is a guaranteed food supply will animals reproduce.

You might be thinking that since we evolved to eat animals it is still okay to eat them. My take on this is that it took hundreds of thousands of years for humans to develop teeth and the digestive tracts that we have today. This occurred long before we began factory farming animals and domesticating wheat, long before our life expectancy doubled in the last one hundred years[29], long before the age of knowledge that we are presently in. Evolution in humans simply does not occur fast enough to respond to our present way of eating.

Our food supply is certain. We don't have to lie in wait for two days to catch a mammoth. Nor do we have to migrate to forests in the spring to feed on bountiful berries.

We have the opportunity now to investigate how we live and how it affects other animals and the planet. Just because we have the physiology to eat other animals does not mean we should do so. There are many studies that show a plant-based diet is more beneficial than a meat diet. The maladies that plague the western world are reduced. Vegans suffer fewer diseases such as heart disease and hypertension because of the absence of animal fats, less incidence of migraines because of the absence of typical triggers, cheese and chocolate. In mood profiles and depression tests vegans score well. Other studies show lower rates of cholesterol, type 2 diabetes and some types of cancer.[30] And of course there is a natural weight loss that comes with not pumping your body full of sugar and fat.

Clothes and Accessories

By now you will be attuned to what you consume. Of course consumption doesn't just mean what we eat. We have spent our lives, for instance, listening to marketers tell us that genuine leather means quality. Famous brands have built reputations on such claims, but is it ethical for vegans to choose leather?

I think individuals need to assess what is in their wardrobe. For me, I have two leather belts. They would be close to thirty years old, so I acquired them long before I became vegan. True to say I would not purchase a leather belt now, but nor am I going to dispose of the two belts because then I would have to replace them and I don't want to be purchasing items unnecessarily which in the end adds to my carbon footprint, since the items need to be manufactured.

As a vegan making a purchasing decision, you can see a lot of thought goes into the purchase. And that's a good thing don't you think? After all, we worked for that money and it's a darn good bargaining tool. Our dollar is our vote for ethical products.

Here are some points to contemplate:

- Consider converting to veganism but know why you are doing it

- Purchase food ethically; organic, free range

- Support SPCA Blue Tick pig and chicken products

- Sign petitions that call for better treatment of commercially farmed animals

- Implement meat-free days

- Implement vegan days

- Support farmers' markets

- Begin experimenting with vegan recipes

11

Environmentalism

"If you want to be perfect, go and sell all your possessions and give money to the poor, and you will have treasure in heaven. Then come, follow me." Jesus (Matthew 19:12)

The environment could be your driver for becoming a minimalist. Right now there is a strong environmental movement for us to clean up our act. The consequences of the excesses of the last few decades have well and truly manifested themselves and come home to roost. Our seas and rivers are polluted and depleted of stocks, our atmosphere is polluted, and we are causing the extinctions of other species. Young people are pointing out that it is not okay to continue business as usual which is a view that the earth is a supermarket for humans and also a dumping ground.

This chapter is broad and may take you in a surprising direction. Obviously, just becoming a minimalist isn't going to change the world overnight but it is important to recognise that all actions have consequences. A decision is weighed up against all the alternatives and consequences. As environmentalists and minimalists we want to make decisions that result in the least damage to the planet.

Landfills

The problem with owning something is that we will at some point in time need to get rid of it. That becomes a problem of choice. In the first instance the packaging needs to be disposed of. Cardboard boxes seem to be reused and a lot of online shopping is making its way through the post in laminated brown paper bags but often the inside is stuffed with plastic cells or soft plastic filled with air. What was wrong with old newspapers? Plastic is the enemy of the environment. It does not go away. Nothing eats it. It just breaks down into tiny pieces, eventually so tiny you can hardly see it. Then there is the consideration of the item itself; its durability, utility and ultimately where it will end up at the end of its functional life. If I am at a museum I will make use of the entry brochure while I am there but return it to the admission counter on the way out. I feel guilty keeping it knowing I have to recycle it. The museum can reuse it. Unfortunately admission to the cinema involves exchanging money for a small paper ticket which is then ripped in half with one half given back to you. Even this bothers me now. It seems to be a tradition harking back to the days of silent movies. On its own one small ticket isn't much, but added to the billions of tickets purchased each day it is an enormous waste of paper, ink, time and transport costs. Extrapolate that out to trees harvested, transported, milled and pulped and the energy resources to facilitate that process, ink cartridges made of plastic designed to be disposed of, andtrucks on the roads spewing carbon dioxide and diesel particulates into our already carbon-soaked atmosphere.

Before I accept anything I consider how I will dispose of it. I loathe gifts for this very problem. For your future reference minimalists prefer food and flowers. Anything else will throw them into ethical turmoil. I have another reason for not liking gifts and I can track this reason to long before I became a minimalist. Anything new had to live somewhere and this upsets the careful balance that I had taken pains to achieve. On reflection, perhaps I've always been a minimalist in the making.

I recently purchased a vacuum cleaner. I did not want the box. The salesperson didn't want the box. He tried really hard to get me to take the box as "it has attachments in it." I was adamant. "It's only a vacuum cleaner," I replied as I covered his counter with cardboard packers, plastic bags and the great big box. He seemed more shocked than bemused but I was happy that I had transferred the problem of disposing the excess packaging onto the seller. For me, the alternative was too taxing. I would have had to find all the plastic grade triangles to put the plastic in the correct recycling receptacle, and break down the cardboard to stuff it in my recycling bin. Such a nuisance.

Every single thing we buy or use is disposed of sooner or later. Imagine that the council rubbish collectors have gone on strike for a year. You face the task of dealing with your own household waste. You are forced to take responsibility for this, perhaps for the first time ever in your life. Will you stockpile it? Unlikely, unless you treat each component differently. You dedicate a corner of the yard for recycling; a large bin each for clean tins, plastics, paper and card. Perhaps this is delegated to the garage, or on the small balcony of an apartment. There is a compost heap near the vegetable garden. If you are not fortunate enough to have a vegetable garden, perhaps you have a worm farm, for those hungry critters will transform organic waste into liquid fertiliser which you can gift to friends who do keep gardens. They will reward you with fresh produce. There is also a bin for waste that won't recycle. All your rubbish will be clean since there is no one to collect it and you have to store it for a long time. You don't want to attract vermin, mosquitoes, wild cats and dogs or flies to lay their eggs and produce maggots.

What I've described is a mini Earth waste system. But we are not so kind to Earth. There is an adage, "Everyone's responsibility is no one's responsibility". In the above scenario we are forced to think about how we deal with the waste we generate. It becomes apparent that unless we dispose of materials responsibly they will pile up to bury us. We quickly learn that the only way to reduce waste is to reduce consumption, or change consumption habits.

The Earth is a closed system. This means that nothing disappears, it just gets shuffled around. You will have heard of the carbon cycle, the oxygen cycle and the nitrogen cycle. Carbon, oxygen and nitrogen are elements in the atmosphere that move between earth's biological systems such as plants and animals including humans, and the air. They are called cycles because everything that is used continues to be used. It cycles round and a balance is maintained. And if something goes skewiff a new equilibrium will be found.

We can apply this cycling concept to the goods we use. More thought is required as to what we purchase so that more of our waste does not end up in a landfill. Reduce, reuse and recycle should be our mantra. And it should be in that order. Recycling should be the last option, after something has well and truly done its dash and is of absolutely no use to anyone. We don't use anything without there being a consequence. The fast food container you threw in the bin doesn't just magically disappear because you disposed of it. You may have very conscientiously placed the coffee cup in the recycle bin but Styrofoam is simply expanded polystyrene and does not recycle. Nor is it biodegradable. In other words it does not break down into carbon, hydrogen or oxygen to be consumed by bacteria. Worms won't eat it either. It will end up in a landfill. Make sure you are being given cardboard coffee cups. However your responsibility does not end there. The plastic lid has a "6" written in the triangle on the lid. This means it is actually really hard to recycle and will end up in a landfill even though you thought you had disposed of it responsibly. Happily there is a wave of consciousness sweeping cities where customers are encouraged to fill their own glass cups. At the end of this chapter is a list of what we cannot recycle. It is shocking. If this does not turn you into a minimalist nothing will. The short story is consuming fewer products results in less waste going to landfills.

Landfill is just a nicer word for rubbish dump. When you put your rubbish bag out at the roadside each week do you consider for one minute where that bag is going? And the fact that the bag is plastic? Or how many other bags there are on the rubbish truck? They go to a big hole in the ground. First they get crushed down at a refuse centre which doesn't sound half as incriminating as "rubbish dump" but make no mistake your waste goes to a big hole in the ground.

In April 2019 after a week of intense rainfall, rubbish from an old landfill near Fox Glacier in Westland, New Zealand began to wash up on the beaches. The coastline was strewn thickly with rubbish for one hundred kilometres and included debris as small as bottle caps and as large as car parts. Local people tried to collect as much of the offending rubbish as possible but much of the coast is inaccessible. It was a tragedy for marine life.

No one would have foreseen this event when it was decided to build the landfill decades ago. But West coast communities occupy a sinuous slither of land wedged between the Southern Alps and the

Tasman Sea. Rainfall runoff is intense and sudden as river catchments fill quickly. Recently rainstorm events have been severe and the sodden ground around the landfill collapsed under these environmental pressures.

New Zealanders sent 2.46 million tonnes of waste to landfills in 2011.[1] That is roughly the equivalent of 2.46 million small city cars or 351, 428 elephants if you like to think in elephants. That was down from 3.15 million tonnes in 2006 before recycling became a buzzword. You might be pleased to think the downward trend has continued but unfortunately the volume of waste isn't tracking down at the same rate.[2]

We consume 735,000 kilograms of packaging. That is more or less equivalent to 735,000 Hyundai Accents or 105,000 elephants and that is on top of the roughly 145,000 vehicles that get scrapped each year. Thankfully not the entire amount of packaging we consume ends up in landfills with approximately 58% being recycled.[2]

When confronted with volumes this large it is hard to imagine that a single individual can make a positive change. Let's break it down into bite-sized chunks. To put this in perspective the total waste produced in a year, 2.46 million tonnes equates to more or less 518 kg per person. That's half a small car. That's just the waste that hits the landfill, not that which gets recycled. When you break it down like that your mind is able to handle it. You can actually relate what you do as having an impact. Suddenly the waste problem is something you can tackle. After all, if you only have to prevent the equivalent of half a small car going to the landfill you can take steps to really make a difference.

The Chemistry of Landfills

What is wrong with burying waste? A lot actually; from the gases released into the atmosphere, and the toxins that leach into the groundwater beneath landfills. Let's start with the gases since we're familiar with the term greenhouse gases. We'll get to the effects of landfill gases in the atmosphere shortly, but first we need to look at landfills.

Landfills produce toxic gases. The big four are methane, carbon dioxide, ammonia and sulfides, with methane and carbon dioxide comprising 90-98% of the total. The gases are produced when bacteria break down waste. These gases can continue to be expelled some fifty years after a landfill has closed. We can't just keep tossing our waste into the ground. One small action today has a cumulative effect on the future.

At this point we need to understand the oxygen, carbon and nitrogen cycles. Below is a really cute diagram of how the oxygen and carbon cycles.

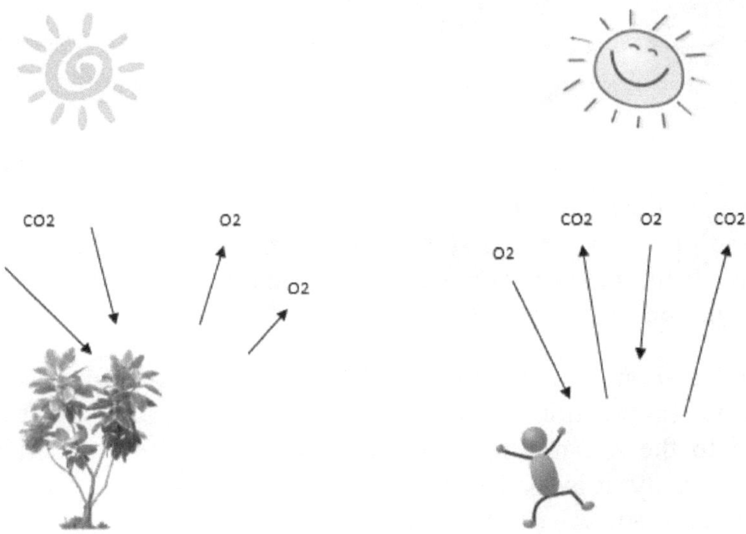

During the day plants take in carbon dioxide and expel oxygen. Plants need the sun to convert the carbon dioxide into food. Oxygen is taken up by other living things such as us, and we breathe out carbon dioxide. But that's a bit too simple. Let's take a look at the oxygen cycle in a bit more detail.

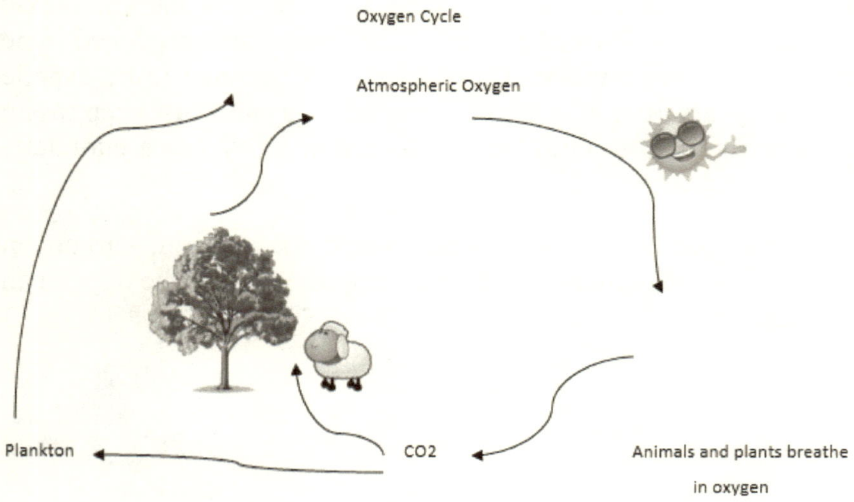

Oxygen is continuously used and created by living organisms. It is created in two ways: firstly by plants. This is why deforestation is bad. No plants means no oxygen for anyone. Oxygen is also created by sunlight via a reaction it has with water vapour.

Oxygen is used in respiration. We can't breathe without it. It is used in decomposition. A body will not decompose without being exposed to the air, nor will steel rust. It's not called oxidation for nothing. Finally, it is used in combustion. Have you ever tried to light a fire with not enough draft to get it going?

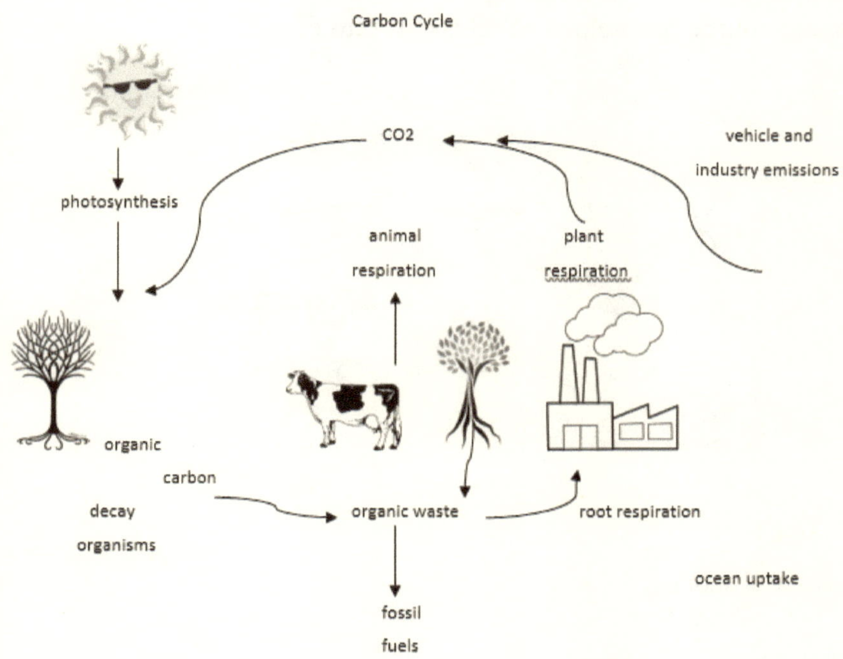

Carbon dioxide is continuously removed from and added to the atmosphere. As at 5 April 2019 there were four hundred and twelve parts per million of carbon dioxide up there.[3] This is sucked up by all living things as we breathe. But there is oodles of it locked up. Firstly, the oceans act as big sponges taking as much carbon dioxide as is necessary to sustain the life of the animals in the ocean that depend upon it. It also takes up a surplus. The ocean has been a dumping ground as more carbon dioxide has hit the atmosphere. The other place carbon dioxide goes to is into the ground in the form of animal waste and organic material. Anything that has ever lived and died has carbon in it. As a matter of interest, carbon dating works because when we die we stop taking up carbon. It gets set at the time of termination.

There are a couple of points to note in the above diagram. Vehicle and industry emissions add a lot to the natural balance of the cycle. Where did the source for these emissions come from? Fossil fuels of course: oil and gas. Incidentally, fossil simply mean

145

something that has been dug up. Unlocking the carbon dioxide from this giant source has helped to release it into the air.

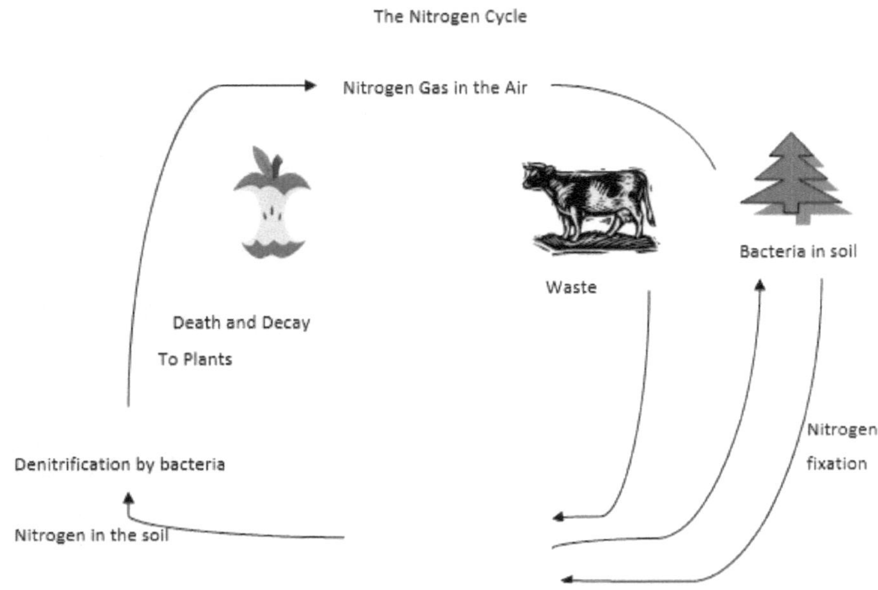

Nitrogen makes up seventy eight percent of the air but it is useless to us in its gaseous state. The natural process is that specialised bacteria in the soil "fix" the nitrogen and transform it into ammonium and nitrate so the plant can utilise the nitrogen as a protein. This makes chlorophyll which is used in photosynthesis to make food for the plant. Other bacteria do the reverse, and the transformation of nitrogen into those two component parts and back again is the nitrogen cycle. In the old days clover was one such plant that farmers used to rely on to fix nitrogen in the soil. If a paddock was lush with clover there would be good grass growth. Since 1913 however, the Haber Bosch nitrogen fixing process has allowed the wholesale production of nitrogen fertiliser and the exponential production of global food crops, but, as we have seen, that's another story altogether.

From the above you can see how even the smallest things that we use are cycled. The most essential elements that we can't even see and which keep us alive cycle endlessly. Nothing disappears. The earth is a closed system, the ultimate efficient recycling system.

Unfortunately landfills provide unique environments for certain chemical reactions. People aren't fussy about what they dispose of: organic waste is mixed with recyclable metals and toxin-producing plastics. Over time and under the weight of waste material landfills becomes anaerobic. This means no oxygen and therefore no oxygen cycles.

Other anaerobic environments include rice paddies and swamps. All the fossil fuels that we now use were formed in the Cretaceous period, 80-64 million years ago, from anaerobic swamps. Oil was once tonnes of plant matter compressed in oxygen deprived swamps – that means lots of carbon. Let's look at the chemicals in a little more depth.

Since there is no oxygen the most lethal gas released from landfills is methane, chemical symbol CH_4. It looks like this:

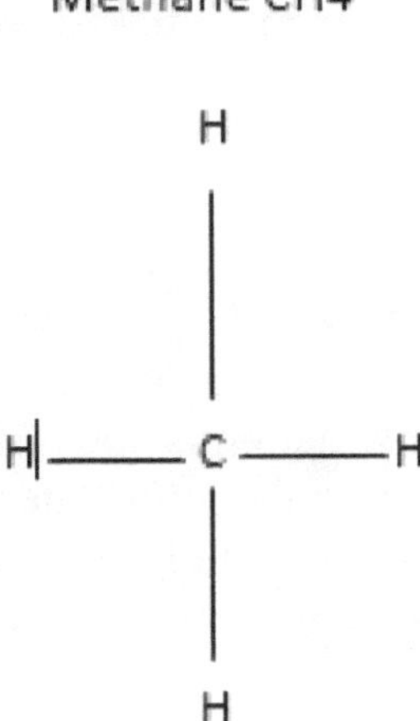

It has one carbon atom with four hydrogen atoms attached. It is a greenhouse gas which means it absorbs the sun's heat and therefore warms the atmosphere. In the first two decades after its release, methane is eighty six times more potent than carbon dioxide. Therefore it warms the planet eighty six times more than carbon dioxide. After that it decays to carbon dioxide. Landcare Research notes that methane is New Zealand's largest contributor to all our gas emissions.[4]In fact globally we have the highest rate per capita of methane emissions at 0.6 tonnes per person per year. One third of this emanates from ruminant animals such as sheep and cattle. According to the Ministry for the Environment's annual calculations this has increased ten percent since 1990. Methane is a flammable gas. Along with carbon dioxide these two gases make up to ninety to ninety eight percent of all landfill gases. The peak gas release occurs at around seven years but landfills will continue to release gases for over fifty years.[5]

There are over four hundred landfills in New Zealand which are regulated by the Ministry for the Environment.[6] One method to try to reduce the amount of waste ending up in landfills has been to levy all waste. You will have noticed that there is even a charge for disposing of green waste at refuse stations now. It is however free to dump your filled council rubbish bag since you already paid a levy in purchasing the bag. You might like to lobby your local council to swap the environmentally unfriendly plastic rubbish bags for paper kleensaks. At least these will break down quickly, returning the carbon and nitrogen to the ground.

NH3Ammonia

Ammonia is the gas form of ammonium. It's emitted from landfills from the decay of rotting organic matter. The Ministry for the Environment calculates that emissions have increased twenty-five percent since 1990.[7] Ammonia contributes to the formation of acid rain. In fact the molecule looks a bit like an umbrella.

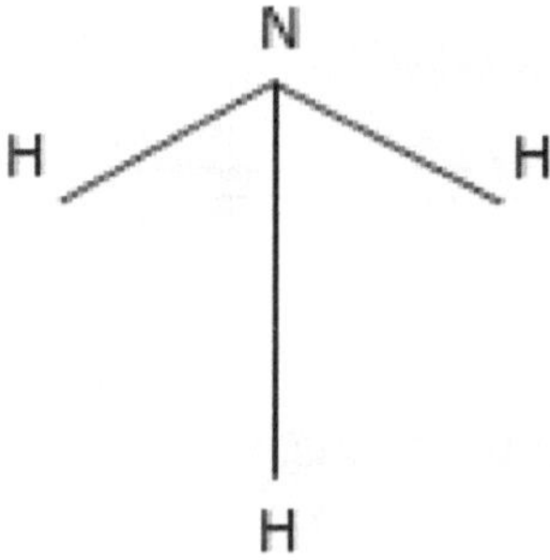

H2SHydrogen Sulfide

The amount of hydrogen sulphide released depends upon the amount of moisture in the landfill and its temperature. It is the breakdown of organic waste that creates hydrogen sulphide, so once again, you have to stop those lazy work colleagues from dumping their unwanted fries in the bin. We all know that it ends up in a plastic bag and going to the landfill. Bad! Here is what it looks like.

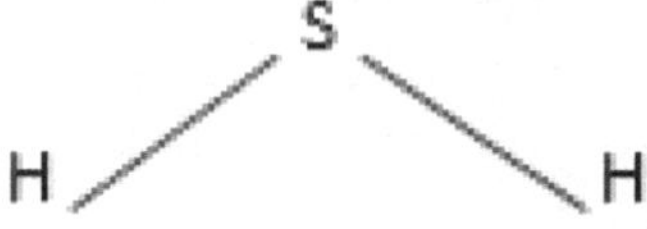

This is the classic rubbish dump smell, a bit like rotten eggs. Love it or hate it. It's the gas that's released from volcanoes, swamps and natural gas. It occurs from microbial breakdown in anaerobic conditions. Man-made sources are sewers and landfills. It has one sulphur atom and two hydrogen atoms.

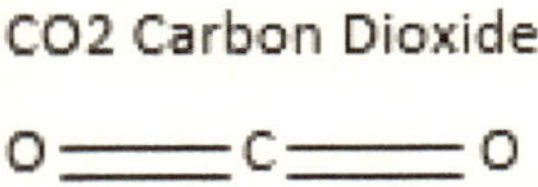

Note the double bonds in this molecule. It means the bond is stronger between oxygen and carbon but conversely it is less stable due to a greater amount of reactivity compared to a single bond. Carbon dioxide in the atmosphere acts as a greenhouse gas. It is derived from volcanic activity and the combustion of organic material and it cycles in the respiration of living organisms.

The problem with carbon dioxide being released into the atmosphere is that it helps to trap heat. The heat that normally dissipates back to space at night is unable to escape and therefore heats the earth.

Leaching from Landfills

We've seen how gases emitted from landfills affect the air. Now let's turn our attention to what's going on beneath a landfill. We've all seen rubbish dumps. People don't care what gets biffed in them; heavy metals, organic waste, plastic. And they always stink. Landfills are exposed to the open air, rain and sunshine.

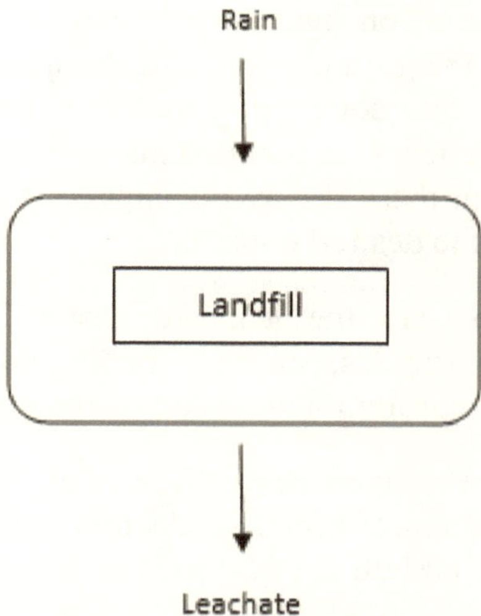

Rain saturates the rubbish. As the rainwater percolates through the rubbish it promotes decomposition by bacteria and fungi. These tiny organisms love the damp. This activity sucks up all the available oxygen to produce an anoxic environment. The temperature within the rubbish heap rises and pH falls so the rainwater becomes very acidic. It is easier for metal ions to dissolve in this contaminated water. PH is a measure of how acidic or alkaline a liquid is. Leachate is the term used to describe the contaminant that has originated from the landfill.

The leachate is able to react easily with materials which under normal conditions would not be reactive, for example, cement or gypsum based building materials, thereby changing the chemical composition. When the leachate percolates into the groundwater, contaminants can travel well beyond the rubbish dump as the water flows away.

Initially leachate is black but as it oxygenates it becomes yellow or brown and quickly develops a bacterial flora. Perfect conditions for the incubation of disease causing pathogens such as viruses and bacteria but also for fungi, protozoa and worms.

Nowadays it is common practice to treat leachate. Modern landfills are constructed on huge membranes which are designed to limit toxins entering the groundwater. The dump should also contain a leachate drainage system comprising multiple filtering levels. At the collection sump the leachate is pumped into treatment tanks where the pH is modified. From there it may be shipped to a sewage treatment plant, depending on the desired outcome.

So what exactly are the leachate nasties? Carbon, nitrogen, chloride, phenols, pesticides, solvents, pathogens and heavy metals such as iron, copper, chromium, lead and manganese.

Anything that ever lived has carbon in it. Food, garden waste, paper, timber; typical landfill rubbish. As this organic waste is broken down by bacteria the carbon is released into the atmosphere as carbon dioxide and methane. Normally carbon gets locked up in plants but is released quickly by respiration. But the carbon stuck in a landfill only gets released very slowly.

Nitrogen is another element that likes to hang out with oxygen. As part of the natural nitrogen cycle, when nitrogen gets into the soil via manure the soil doesn't absorb the excess nitrogen which by now has combined with three oxygen atoms to be called nitrate. Now the nitrogen is able to leach away with drainage water. This means it gets into the groundwater which finds its way to streams and finally the ocean. While it's hanging around streams and ponds it over-stimulates the plant growth. Rampant plant growth in aquatic environments leads to clogging up the water intake, sucking up the available oxygen in the water as the plants decompose and the blocking of light to deeper water. This all leads to an anaerobic pond or stream and dead fish.

Chloride has its good and bad points depending on what it is used for. During World War I it was used as a chemical weapon. It is used to kill bacteria and make water clean, even for drinking water. But it is poisonous. In South America some frogs have a little atom of it in their skin. Indians used to dip the tips of their spears onto the frog. The frogs probably thought they were onto a good thing until the humans cottoned on. Another bad thing; chloride destroys the ozone.

Phenols are organic compounds comprising C6H6OH. Put simply think mildly acidic disinfectant.

Most pesticides stick to soil particles, particularly to nice sticky clay which prevents the pesticide from leaching into groundwater. But some pesticides don't. If pesticides make it into the groundwater, without a flushing mechanism they are going to stay there for a long time and not dilute.

Then there is a range of metals. Naturally soil contains some very useful metals such as iron, copper and manganese, but when there is more of these than the soil can accommodate then that is disastrous for plants. Metal polluted soils will not grow good healthy crops. Plants will be sickly and weak.

If landfills are bad for the environment and we keep building more of them you would be forgiven for thinking there is no alternative. However the news is good. It is becoming common practice in some countries to build energy plants from all the rubbish that a country generates. These are massive waste disposal complexes that incinerate at over eight hundred and fifty degrees. We are not talking recycle but disposal of the stuff we can't use again. There are over two thousand Waste to Energy plants worldwide and Sweden has thirty three of them.[8]

Emissions are scrubbed so the nasties described above are not dissipated into the air. The ash that results from the burning is sieved for metals and the slag is used in road construction. A stunning example of a recently constructed Waste to Energy plant is the one in Copenhagen, Denmark. The building is not an ugly warehouse located on the edge of the city where you might expect to see such a heavy industrial plant. No. it is planted smack bang in the middle of the city. The stunning design is such that the people take pride in it and it doubles its use as a ski slope. That's how big this plant is. Architecturally it is pleasing, with a shape a bit like a swirl. It's white and incorporates vegetation into the walls.

The plant receives four hundred thousand tonnes of water per annum and is ninety nine percent efficient. It recovers ninety percent of all metals amounting to ten thousand tonnes per annum. One hundred thousand tonnes of ash is produced which is used in road construction. This can save mining for gravel.

But that's not all. The incineration of all this waste heats one hundred and twenty thousand homes and provides electricity for a further sixty two and a half thousand homes.[9]

In New Zealand the West Coast is being mooted as a site for such a plant and resource consents are being prepared. However, these plants are super expensive and New Zealand is slow to get on board because of this. But with environmentally aware interest groups such as the Green Party in Germany pushing to completely ban landfilling by 2020 we should consider the alternatives no matter the financial cost. The planet relies on us to finally do the right thing.

In New Zealand we get away with many environmentally unsound practices because we don't suffer population pressures. If we had seventy million people as the United Kingdom does our landscape would be full to bursting with rubbish. We have the chance to be mindful of our beautiful land before we overpopulate it.

Overpopulation

Humans are good at breeding and just like other animals we breed more when there are plenty of resources to support our offspring. Only ten thousand years ago there were a few million people across the entire planet. By the early eighteen hundreds we clocked up our first billion. But it only took one hundred and twenty years to double it. That's right. By the nineteen twenties the human population was two billion. The US Census Bureau notes that in 1960 three billion people were alive, in 1974 there were four billion, in 1987 there were five billion, in 1999 there were six billion and in 2011 there were seven billion. The United Nations has June 2019 at seven and a half billion people and predicts the human population in 2050 at nine point seven billion and in 2100 at eleven billion.

Year	Population
1804	1 billion
1927	2 billion
1960	3 billion
1974	4 billion
1987	5 billion
1999	6 billion
2011	7 billion
2019	7.5 billion

(US Census Bureau)

There is a downward trend in fertility rates. The UN Population Division notes that from 1970-1975 women were having 4.7 babies compared to 2005-2010 when they were having 2.6 babies. On the table above we can see that the time period between billions of humans produced over time becomes less, although the projection for 2019 looks to buck this trend. Many Western countries cannot even achieve replacement rate so this probably has some significance.

It will be interesting to see if the rate does slow as predicted. Not everyone is able to access services to reproductive health. In some countries there is no such thing. World Population Day is a United Nations initiative that came out of a 1989 international conference where 179 governments recognised that reproductive health and gender equality are essential for achieving sustainability. Without this, women are little more than baby factories adding to the already burgeoning human population whether they want to or not.

As environmentalists and minimalists we don't want to create a bigger footprint than we already do. That footprint depends on how much we consume. We can use carbon dioxide output as a measure of a country's consumption. People living in low and middle income countries consume little and therefore make less impact on the environment. But as these people become wealthier they will consume more. Burgeoning middle classes demand high energy derived food such as milk and meat and wealthy countries such as New Zealand are more than happy to sell it to them.

Does that make the consumers responsible for the emissions created in the manufacturing of products, or the manufacturers? Without demand there would be no manufacturing. If we didn't shop in those cheap $2.00 shops the creation of cheap junk would reduce. If we stopped buying fast food big corporate chain stores would quickly go out of business. You can see that a change in consumption habits will greatly impact the environment.

Global Warming

At the beginning of this discussion I used illustrations to show how the greenhouse gases cycle. They regulate the planet at a constant temperature. Water vapour, methane, ozone, nitrous oxide and halocarbons, that is, chemicals where one or more carbon atoms are linked to one or more halogen atoms, all play a part in absorbing and emitting heat from the sun as it enters the atmosphere to warm the earth and from the earth as it emits excess heat back into space.

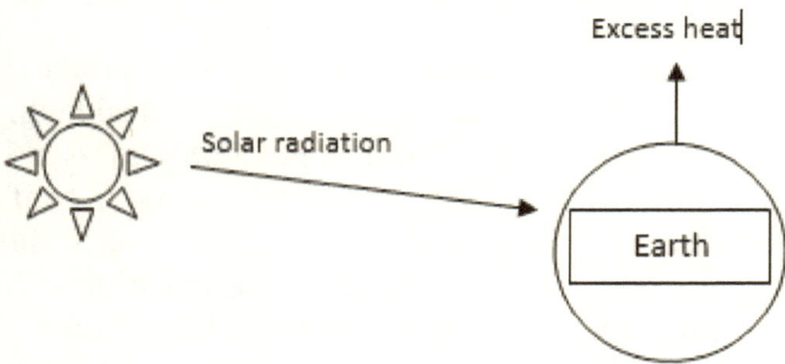

We can measure the amount of carbon dioxide in the atmosphere from analyzing ice cores. Pre-industrial revolution, the carbon dioxide content was 270 parts per million (ppm).[10] There are various ways that scientists measure carbon dioxide, but climate scientists who

156

measure atmospheric carbon dioxide count the number of carbon dioxide molecules in a given number of molecules in the air after water vapour has been removed. Therefore, 270 ppm of carbon dioxide means that in every million molecules of dry air there are on average 270 carbon dioxide molecules. Since the industrial revolution we have been burning coal, oil and gas mined from the ground. This has released carbon into the atmosphere which bonds with oxygen thus increasing the amount of carbon dioxide. The consequence is that more heat is trapped in the atmosphere.

The coal and oil dates to the Cretaceous, 80-64 million years ago. Coal is the product of layers and layers of higher plant species such as tree ferns and tropical plants buried in swamps and compressed over millions and millions of years. The degree of pressure and temperature over that time resulted in four grades of coal that we recognise today. Therefore, coal is a land-based product made from fossil vegetation.

Oil, on the other hand, is a marine or lake-based product. It comprises algae, plankton, bacteria and simple organisms buried in sandstone or limestone deposits. Oil therefore, is fossilised aquatic animals.

Coal and oil took approximately sixteen million years to make at around the time the dinosaurs were here. The planet has had sixty three million years to deal with the effect of having all that carbon and oxygen locked up. Sixty three million years is an extraordinary length of time for a system to develop a new equilibrium. Now humans have altered that state. The industrial revolution has thrown a huge spanner in the works. The gases that we've unlocked have to go somewhere. They don't disappear just because we can't see them. They dissipate into the atmosphere where they attract moisture and absorb infrared radiation. Incidentally, the industrial revolution probably hasn't contributed to the whole increase. It is observed that we've been adding carbon dioxide to the atmosphere from at least the start of our foray into widespread agriculture some nearly ten thousand years ago. Rice paddies are one culprit that add greenhouse gases so we really have been altering the atmosphere for thousands of years.

In a greenhouse scenario the excess heat that normally emits back to space gets trapped with the effect that the whole planet warms up. Imagine you spoon some warm soup into a plastic container and you put the lid on before the soup has cooled. The excess heat cannot escape and the lid fogs up. Global warming looks just like that.

What if you take the lid off or poke a hole in the lid? Yes. The soup would cool quicker and the lid wouldn't gain as much condensation. So, can that explanation apply to the earth? Aha. The planet has the ozone layer. And it does have a hole in it. Slightly more heat can escape through the hole which is situated in the stratosphere above Antarctica during spring. But it is not a flash idea to increase the size of the hole because the ozone layer shields us from harmful ultraviolet rays that come from the sun.

On 23 March 2018,carbon dioxide in the atmosphere measured 409.57 ppm and on 23 March 2019 it measured 410.95ppm, as measured at the Mauna Loa Observatory in Hawaii (NOAA-ESRL).[11]The last time Earth experienced anything like those levels was during a warm period in the mid Pliocene which extended 5.3 million to 2.65 million years ago. Carbon dioxide was 350-450 ppm. We know this from analysing fossils in sedimentary cores. Prior to this the earth was awash with atmospheric carbon dioxide during the Cretaceous, and at the boundary of the Paleocene and the Eocene, 56 million years ago.

For now we will travel back to the mid Pliocene, for it gives a good indicator as to what the Earth can expect from having high levels of carbon dioxide in the atmosphere. This was a time of forests in the Arctic and Antarctic and large mammals roamed the land. Temperatures were possibly nineteen degrees Celsius higher in the Arctic than today. This warmth may have triggered changes in global ocean circulation, which precipitated the melting of the Greenland and Antarctic ice sheets. Sea levels were much higher.

We can expect these changes to occur again hundreds and thousands of years into the future. There is an approximate five million cubic miles of ice on earth and scientists estimate it would take five thousand years to fully melt. Seas would rise seventy metres. Change is already afoot. The Arctic is currently warming faster than the rest of the planet. This is termed polar amplification. This happened during the Pliocene too. Fire was widespread through those northern forests and lately Siberia, Alaska and Greenland have had significant fires.[12] Right now we are seeing an influx of polar bears on land as sea ice melts. This forces interaction with humans as they look for food. I fear for the outcome of these first bears as they try to adapt to the new norm.

There is always a lag in a system. It takes time for a process to kick in. This is why a carbon dioxide rich atmosphere now will have devastating consequences in the future. Have you noticed how midday is not the hottest time of the day? It's around three o'clock or later. Have you noticed how the coldest winter month is not around the solstice, the shortest day, but six to eight weeks later? These are simple examples of systems that have lags. We can readily comprehend this because our observance of the lag effects occurs over a relatively short time span. It's a bit tougher to get our heads around millions of years.

The planet is now 0.8 degrees Celsius warmer than it was in 1880.[13] However, two thirds of that increase has been since 1975. This equates to an increase of between 0.15 and 0.20 degrees Celsius per decade. That is one degree over fifty years. That may sound insignificant but consider this: one degree Celsius represents all the energy that is required to heat the oceans, land and the atmosphere. A mere one to two degrees decrease was enough to trigger the Little Ice Age which lasted from approximately 1350 to 1850. And a five percent drop triggered the last ice age, some 20,000 years ago.[14]It is possible that before we altered the atmosphere and warmed things up we were on track to go back into ice age. That would have been the norm. A feature of the Pliestocene, or the last one million eight hundred thousand years, is the near regular fluctuations in and out of ice ages. Normally the earth would have been longer in ice age than in the intervening years, the interglacials. However, it is now thought that we've gone so far to warm the planet there is no chance of going back into ice age. One of the things required for going into ice age is the northern hemisphere summer temperatures to not rise above freezing for several years. The snow would accumulate and compress into ice sheets. Clearly this is not happening.

Arguments against the idea of global warming point out that the earth has been warmer in the past and that the present warming is just part of a natural cycle. We know the planet has been warmer. There were once trees in the Antarctic. But it took millions of years for the Antarctic to become the ice continent we know today. It took so long in fact that one of the drivers was the creation of the southern ocean due to plate boundary movements. Without the tectonics plates rifting to form the southern ocean there would be no great frozen continent. Plate boundaries move typically one to four millimetres per annum with some occasional speedy ones at ten millimetres per annum. So you can see that changes are slow and take millions

of years. The difference with the changes occurring at the moment is the fast rate of temperature change. Science can pin it on one factor: human activity. It is indisputable that the actions of man have contributed to the warming of the planet and it is indisputable that we began to make a big difference since the age of steam.

The earth is experiencing climate upheaval and we are witnessing increased intensity and more frequent storm events. With an increase in atmospheric moisture content (remember the lid with condensation on it) the air becomes warmer. Climate modelling predicts that for a two degree Celsius warming scenario rainfall rates will increase ten to fifteen percent and cyclone intensities will increase one to ten percent.[15]

Hurricanes form over warm seas. Heating of the oceans will intensify tropical storm wind speeds which are more destructive when they make landfall. We can expect a two to eleven percent increase in average maximum wind speed as well as more of these intense storms. Warmer oceans will see up to twenty percent more precipitation.[15]Rainy days ahead.

It is possible that you are wondering what this has to do with living minimally. As a species the way we live unsustainably, continually taking everything this planet has to offer without giving anything in return, has direct consequences for the future of Earth and for the future of our species. Everything we do has consequences. When we make the decision to live minimally we must weigh up the consequences of the choices we make. This can take us to unexpected

160

places. If all 7.5 billion people had the freedom to make such sustainable choices we might slow the rate of climate warming. Only when we understand the consequences of our actions will we be motivated to make a change.

Extinctions

The planet has previously undergone five global extinctions. Humans had not evolved to witness a single one of them. The first is referred to as the Ordovician-Silurian Extinction. It occurred four hundred and thirty nine million years ago. This was huge. Eighty six percent of life was wiped out. Most life at this time was aquatic. There were enormous amounts of plants which sucked out all the carbon dioxide from the air which in turn raised the temperature. At the same time falling sea levels occurred due to the rise of the Appalachians. Remember the speed of the tectonic plates? This mountain building took millions of years. Less sea equals more land equals more vegetation sucking up carbon dioxide. Luckily a wonderful group of animals called trilobites survived.

The second major extinction was the late Devonian Extinction. This occurred three hundred and sixty four million years ago. Seventy five percent of life on earth was lost. It is possible that giant land plants may have been the catalyst. With huge deep roots lots of nutrients were released into the oceans which promoted algal blooms. As these blooms deplete the oceans of oxygen, the animal life in the oceans which were dependent on oxygen, died off. It is thought that land animals were killed off by the ash fallout from volcanic eruptions.

Then there was the biggie. The Permian-Triassic Extinction occurred two hundred and fifty one million years ago and a staggering ninety six percent of life was exterminated. Enormous volcanic eruptions filled the air with carbon dioxide and there was a surplus of methane emitting bacteria. The earth warmed and oceans became acidic. Incredibly, all life today evolved from the four percent of life that survived this extinction.

The most dramatic extinction was the Triassic-Jurassic Extinction which occurred two hundred and one million years ago over an eighteen million year period. It was the result of asteroid impact, climate change and massive flood basalt eruptions. Over fifty percent of living species completely died out.

But the most famous of all the extinctions is the one which wiped the magnificent dinosaurs off the face of the earth. This is known as the Cretaceous-Paleogene Extinction and it occurred sixty five million years ago. It ended seventy six percent of life. Again, asteroid impact, volcanic activity and climate change is thought to have been the catalyst.[16]

Extinction	Years Ago
Ordovician-Silurian	439 million
Devonian	364 million
Permian-Triassic	251 million
Triassic-Jurassic	201 million
Cretaceous-Paleogene	65 million

It is tempting to dismiss extinction as something that is a natural part of earth's cycles, that we have no control over extinctions. Humans have been around for but the blink of an eye, geologically speaking, and everywhere we go we effect change. We even wiped out our early cousins, the Neanderthals, when we encountered them.[17] Of course we did a little breeding with them first. We know this because all descendents from European Caucasian stock have some Neanderthal DNA.

It is widely accepted that we are in the midst of the sixth extinction. There is a definition for it: it is that human activity triggers a change in global climate which has increased species extinction to between one thousand and ten thousand times faster than the norm.[18]

In 2018, three bird species were pronounced extinct. Hawaii lost a small songbird called po'ouli, Brazil lost the Alagoas foliage-gleaner and a stunning blue parrot, the spix's Macaw.On the brink of extinction are the vaquita, the world's smallest cetacean. It is a porpoise and only thirty of them are alive, living in the Gulf of California. The Sudan has only two Northern White Rhinoceros. They are female and were too old to breed with the one remaining male which recently died. These extinctions don't make news headlines. They are occurring every week. Insects, butterflies, birds, mammals and reptiles have all been on this planet Earth since before homo sapiens and yet it is because of us that they are dying off.

I'm sure you can remember a time, perhaps when you were a child, or perhaps only a few years ago, frogs or a particular bird species was plentiful. Are they plentiful now? What do you think happened to them? They probably didn't simply move to somewhere else. It's a good bet they died off, perhaps locally, perhaps regionally.

Every species has its own neighbourhood regulated by temperature and of course food availability. For example the polar regions have few species but generally they are fairly big: polar bears, Arctic foxes in the Arctic and penguins in the Antarctic. Temperate regions have more species able to live in fluctuating hot and cold temperatures. The tropics are the most biodiverse regions of the planet. This is where the tiniest of insects carve out an existence in the most specialised of roles without having to colonise a large area. This is where evolution has enabled some species to live completely dependent on other species.

It also means that one small variation in conditions for life can have devastating consequences. The golden toad of the Monteverdan cloud forest of Costa Rica has been quoted as the first species to go extinct due to climate change.[19] Living at fifteen hundred metres above sea level the golden toad had a small population and a limited habitat. It was first discovered in 1964 and declared extinct by 1989. The cause of the population collapse was the proliferation of chytrid fungus which was able to thrive in a drier climate. It is fatal for amphibians. New evidence suggests that a particularly dry spell during El Nino conditions was the driver for the change rather than a change in climate due to global warming. But we could also ask why they didn't become extinct in previous dry El Nino events.

Frogs are seen as an indicator species for climate change. This is because the uptake of oxygen and water through their skin increases concentrations of pollutants. Their life cycle exposes them to water and airborne contaminants. Frogs are certainly not as common as they were fifty years ago.

Astonishingly, five new frog species have been discovered in Madagascar. They range from the size of a grain of rice to the size of a fingernail.[20]Madagascar has three hundred and fifty species of frogs and many of them are tiny. The smallest live approximately two centimetres below the leaf litter surface and they stop croaking when they perceive a threat so they are fiendishly difficult to find. The newly discovered frogs belong to the group of narrow-mouthed frogs and three of them belong to a group entirely new to science.

Their discovery illuminates how much we still don't know about life on earth. It would be tragic for these Madagascan frogs to suffer the same fate as the Costa Rican ones.

An Australian rodent recently made headlines. The Bramble Cay melomys lived on a five hectare island in the Torres Strait near the coast of Papua New Guinea. A cay is a small island comprising sand and the highest point on a cay is not very much above sea level. Beautiful photographs of cays abound in tourist brochures for many holiday destinations.

However, all is not well when the surface is scratched away. The Bramble Cay melomys, a little brown rat, had not been observed since 2009. In 2016 the Queensland Government declared the animal extinct with the State Government declaring the same soon after stating that the rodents' extinction was due to "ocean inundation of the low-lying cay, very likely on multiple occasions, during the last decade, causing dramatic habitat loss and perhaps also direct mortality of individuals." It also acknowledged that the rat was the first mammal to become extinct due to anthropogenic climate change.[21]

The sixth extinction doesn't just refer to those chunky and famous animals that our ancestors knew such as the mammoth and the dodo. Humans have wreaked havoc wherever they've gone, decimating forests as a way of hunting and to clear land for agriculture. This practice wiped many floral and faunal species off the face of the earth. The wholesale slaughter of bison in North America brought the species to near extinction. Only one hundred remained in 1880 down from an estimated thirty million. Some island nations such as New Zealand, Hawaii and Australia have miserable tallies of extinct species. Most New Zealanders wouldn't be aware that the country was home to the largest eagle that ever took to the skies or that fifty centimetre dragonflies prowled the wetlands. Most New Zealanders have never heard about Finsch's duck, the stiff-tailed duck, Hodgen's waterhen, the New Zealand coot or the laughing owl. Unfortunately the list goes on. We can help our resident birds and try to breed up our most vulnerable such as kakapo, kokako, kiwi, whio, kea and kaka as well of dozens of others, but our shorebirds which must fly up to Alaska and Siberia are threatened with severe habitat loss in the Yellow Sea. Our conservation efforts therefore must become collaborative with the countries whose shores our shorebirds visit, stopover and choose for breeding.

World Wildlife Fund for Nature believes we are on target to experience by 2020, a decline in global populations of fish, birds, mammals, amphibians and reptiles of sixty seven percent from 1970 levels.[22]That is a staggering statistic. We are still discovering species, particularly in the deepest oceans and the rich tropical rain forests, and we're killing them faster than we can name them.

The Ministry for the Environment released a report on 17 October 2019 on the current state of New Zealand species. It makes sobering reading. Eighty percent of shorebirds, ninety percent of seabirds and twenty two percent of marine mammals are at risk of, or are threatened with extinction. It noted that marine heat waves killed off kelp in Kaikoura and Lyttleton and new introduced species quickly colonised these areas. Warmer seas affect breeding rates of fish or interrupt breeding altogether.

Ocean Acidification

Up until now the oceans have acted as a carbon sink. They've sucked up the excess carbon dioxide that we have pumped into the air while the great northern boreal forests and the mighty Amazon rainforest, the beating lungs of our planet, have quietly regulated the earth's climate through endless cycling of carbon, oxygen and nitrogen.

But this is changing. The oceans have had enough. There is too much carbon and the oceans are warming up and as they warm they lose the ability to absorb more carbon dioxide. There is a natural thermal expansion that occurs when a molecule of water heats up. It loosens up, jiggles about and generally takes up more room. So far most of the sea-level rise that has occurred is due to thermal expansion. Soon the effects of ice sheet melt into the oceans will show on our coastlines. We can expect to see sea level rise of twenty to forty centimetres by 2060 and up to one hundred centimetres by 2100.

The oceans are becoming acidic. They are now thirty percent more acidic than they were at the beginning of the industrial revolution.[23]The 2019 report by the Ministry for the Environment notes that the pH of waters around New Zealand will decrease, that is, become more acidic. It predicts an increase of 0.3 to 0.4 units by the end of this century and that it will take thousands of years to reverse this.

If we continue at this rate and do absolutely nothing, by the year 2100 the surface waters of the oceans could have acidity levels one hundred and fifty percent higher than the pre-industrial revolution.[23] It would be great for photosynthetic algae and sea grasses but disastrous for calcifying species such as oysters, clams, sea urchins and coral.

In the ocean, carbon dioxide reacts with seawater to form carbonic acid. This causes the acidity of seawater to increase. But the effect of too much carbon dioxide in the oceans is not uniform. The polar regions are experiencing a greater rate of change. This is because carbon dioxide dissolves well in cold water and at present ocean acidification is strongest in the Arctic and Antarctic seas.[24]

We are seeing shellfish that are unable to build strong shells and coral that is dying, bleached, dead. It is estimated that by 2100 only thirty percent of corals will have enough building material for their skeletons. At present some four hundred million people rely on coral for their food and for protection against storm surges.[25]So the absence of coral reefs will impact not only the brightly coloured fish that live amongst them, but the people who rely on fish as a primary food supply. And if by some fortunate circumstance these people survive, living off some land-based resource, the coast will erode in front of their eyes as the storm surges destroy the beaches by sucking the sand out to sea.

Ocean acidification will affect the more than one billion people who rely on a diet of seafood presently and the increased population that we might expect to rely on seafood in the future. If the year 2100 is too far away to contemplate, let's bring it closer to home. If you know of someone who has just had a baby then that baby will probably live long enough to see the year 2100 and they will have witnessed a change not of their own making. They will remember a time when eating seafood was not only a normal thing to do, but was crucial for the survival of large swathes of populations globally. By the year 2100 wars will break out over the resources, and famine will strike populations that presently rely on shellfish.

Deforestation

Deforestation refers to the logging, burning and clearing of indigenous forests. These forests provide habitat for a wide variety of creatures such as insects, birds, mammals and humans. No trees means no regulation of the planet's atmospheric health and the threatened extinction of fauna and flora. The Food and Agriculture Organization of the United Nations monitors global deforestation. The Global Forest Resources Assessment 2015 report notes that since 1990 the rate of forest loss has halved as more forests have come under protection. Since 1990 however, most of the deforestation has occurred in the tropics, where previously it was in Africa and South America.[26]

Forests are razed for different reasons. In some countries the land is used for cattle farming. The danger here is that once the forest cover is removed and cattle move onto the land, the minerals in the soil are very quickly depleted. When it rains, instead of the forest cover letting the water percolate deeply into the soil through the leaf letter and root systems, the rain grabs the soil and pours away, taking precious minerals with it. It only takes three years for the land to be unsuitable for growing grass and supporting cattle so yet more forest is cleared which enables a further three years of cattle farming to occur.

Deforestation causes biodiversity loss and soil erosion. Our soil has taken more than ten thousand years to form. It is formed from weathered bedrock, so depending on the composition of the rock, the soil may be very rich in minerals that plants like to absorb such as the volcanic soils of Auckland and Pukekohe, or they may be very poor such as the soils around the central plateau of the North Island. When raindrops hit an exposed sod of soil it bounces off taking with it a tiny piece of soil. It then flows away with rivulets of other drops of water. Amplify this and you have soil erosion. You can't get it back. As soil it is gone forever. Not only that. Major mudslides are frequent where land has been destabilised due to the removal of forests. After heavy rains great sheets of mud-enriched water surges downhill engulfing villages and claiming hundreds if not thousands of lives. This is a consequence of poorly planned and often illegal deforestation.

In New Zealand great water-laden landslides are not common but we can see the results of deforestation more recently on the Paraparas, the road between Raetihi and Whanganui. This is very steep land and would have been cleared of its indigenous forest cover a hundred or more years ago. In October 2019 a portion of this land developed creep, opening cracks in the ground. Within a week a whole hillside slumped wiping out the road and tumbling into the valley below. As with the Manawatu Gorge, it will take years to repair or install another thoroughfare. Would the land have slumped without the removal of the forest cover? Probably not.

The other important reason indigenous forests are cleared is for the establishment of palm and rubber plantations. One crop agriculture is not the answer. Bugs and viruses love one crop agriculture. It's like a department store for them except they are happy to have only one food choice. They don't need to work to find their food and lay their eggs. They don't even need to shop around. You know how regions are known for the crops they grow? There are entire provinces specialising in either pip or stone fruit, root crops or vineyards. One strain of disease is able to decimate a whole crop. Unfortunately the human solution to this unnatural growing model is to develop and apply insecticides. Take a bicycle tour around some of the above-mentioned areas. Do you see any birds. Any insects?

One crop agriculture can be devastating for the land and towns around it. Take avocados, palm and rubber, for example. All available water goes into making the trees grow. Water is actually diverted to the trees and is literally trucked away inside the crops. Villages, especially in Mexican avocado growing areas, are left without traditional water supplies and have to ship in water to survive. That is bizarre. So actually, some monocrop agriculture practices make deserts of the surrounding area.

Rubber

No prizes for guessing what most of the world's rubber goes into producing. Tyres. A staggering seventy five percent of all rubber produced makes tyres and vehicle numbers have been projected to triple by 2050.[27] What a truly frightening thought.

Rubber was so important to Henry Ford that in 1928 he established a town in the Amazonian rainforest in Brazil, which he named Fordlandia, solely to control the supply of rubber for his motor cars. He found that the British monopoly on Ceylon rubber was increasing the price he was paying for it and he didn't like that.

However, it is not Brazil that supplies most of the world's rubber today, it is Asia with ninety percent of the market. This is a disaster for a relatively small concentrated area as natural forest is razed to the ground to plant rubber trees. To this end the World Wildlife Fund and the Rainforest Alliance work with companies such as General Motors, Michelin, Pirelli and Bridgestone to certify the entire supply chain to ensure sustainable practice as well as workers' rights.

Whilst there is no formal third party accreditation scheme for sustainably and ethically produced rubber, there is the New York Declaration of Forests which was signed at the 2014 Climate Summit by thirty seven countries, sixty three non-governmental organisations and fifty three of the world's largest companies. These organisations pledged to halve the rate of deforestation by 2020, to end it by 2030 and to restore land the size of India.

Unfortunately the goals are not on target to be met. A progress report was published in 2018 by Forest Declaration who noted some of the reasons in the countries most at risk from deforestation. These include weak forest governance, weak laws for breaches, commercial reward from agriculture drives illegal deforestation and that access to forest related information is costly, and not easy to obtain. In addition some major consumer countries are not exerting pressure for an ethical or sustainable rubber industry in the way that has occurred with coffee, cocoa, tea and palm. There is however, education at the grass roots level and there is community awareness. But this is small and people have all the above mentioned issues to tackle.[28]

World Wildlife Fund (WWF) is one agency that works to protect the rainforests of South East Asia. In Southern China it is working with the government to return thousands of hectares of forest land which was destroyed to plant illegal rubber plantations. This was once elephant habitat and there is a plan to restore the land to semi-natural forests.

In Sumatra WWF is working with Michelin to design deforestation-free wildlife friendly plantations that provide income for workers but produce environmentally sustainable rubber.

In Myanmar supply chains are tracked and sustainable rubber production strategies are being developed with the Ministry of Agriculture, the producers' Association and others. Farmers are being educated.

This is not an easy fix. In many situations corruption, land grabbing, human and labour rights violations, illegal logging and deforestation are every day normal life. When consumers of rubber, and that's everyone who owns a car, puts pressure on companies those companies are more likely to set higher standards on the supply chains of their products.

Ecological Footprint

It is difficult to effect change if we don't understand the effects of our current actions. We can measure our consumption against other countries by referring to a global hectare per person (ghpp). This comprises the ecological footprint of people and activities as well as the biocapacity of the earth. One global hectare represents the average productivity of all biologically productive areas measured in hectares on earth in a given year. Think of it as a framework for measuring the human demand on the planet's resources. It is an accounting concept: how fast we are consuming natural resources and how much waste we are generating compared to how fast nature can absorb our waste and generate new resources. The calculation looks like this:

(The planet's biocapacity/humanity's ecological footprint) X demand of 365 days = Earth Overshoot Day

On the demand side is the ecosystems' supply of resources such as timber, fibre, space for urban infrastructure and forests to absorb carbon dioxide. On the supply side is all the biologically productive land, sea area, forests, grazing land, crop land, fishing grounds and built up land.

According to the Living Planet Report New Zealand's current footprint is 4.31 ghpp. Europe's is 4.72 ghpp, Australia 6.68 ghpp, the United States and Canada 7.12ghpp. By contrast African countries average 1.45 ghpp. Over eighty percent of the global population lives in countries running ecological deficits. In other words they use more resources than can be renewed.[29]

New Zealanders live as if we have a spare planet. But we don't have a spare planet to provide the resources that we are presently gobbling through on Earth. You can see that our spending habits are impacting our planet. We are living miles beyond our means. We are borrowing from the future. In fact we are consuming into the next few generations as it will be future generations that have to deal with the excess waste that is denigrating our planet. It will be our grandchildren that have to come up with new ways of living on planet Earth, whether it is by technological innovation or green revolution.

The concept of living beyond our means ecologically is referred to as overshoot. The planet has been in overshoot mode since 1970. Globally we use the equivalent of 1.7 planet earths to provide the resources that we use and absorb our waste. What this means is that it takes over eighteen months to regenerate what we use in one year. We use more ecological services than nature can regenerate. We overfish the oceans faster than fish stocks can breed and we overharvest forests faster than replacement trees can grow. We therefore emit carbon dioxide into the atmosphere faster than forests can recycle it.

Of course there are geological resources that are also not limitless. All metal is mined, all oil is drilled for. These commodities are the result of natural geological forces that happened over millions of years, millions of years ago. They will not come again. They are finite.

Each year Earth Overshoot Day is predicted. In the year 2000 it was in October. In 2017 it was 2 August. In 2018 it was 1 August and in 2019 it was 31 July. This is tracking the wrong way. You can see we are not doing the planet any favours. This date needs to be pushed out, not brought back. We will only get it right when that date is restored to 31 December. So, 31 July 2019 was the day that all of humanity had used the planet's resources that it takes the planet one full year to regenerate. From 31 July to 31 December we were borrowing from the future. As global population increases the earth will reach overshoot day earlier in the year.

The Global Footprint Network lists the top ten countries that are hard on resources:[30]

Country	Global hectares worth of resources consumed per person per annum
1. Kuwait	5.1
2. Australia	4.8
3. United Arab Emirates	4.7
4. Qatar	4.0

5. United States of America   3.9

6. Canada   3.8

7. Sweden   3.8

8. Bahrain   3.6

9. Trinadad & Tobago   3.5

10. Singapore   3.4

The Earth Overshoot day is equally sobering:

1. Qatar   2 February

2. Luxembourg   16 February

3. United Arab Emirates   8 March

4. Kuwait   11 March

5. United States of America   15 March

6. Canada   18 March

7. Denmark   29 March

8. Australia   31 March

9. Sweden   3 April

10. Finland/Belgium/Saudi Arabia   6 April

11. New Zealand   6 May

12. United Kingdom   17 May

This information was retrieved from https://www.overshootday.org

You can calculate your own ecological footprint online to see how many earths you need to sustain your present lifestyle. It certainly is an eye opener. I thought I had a good chance at being one earth or below. Big points in my favour are that I am vegan and drive an electric car. I live in a country where approximately eighty five percent of electricity generated is renewable. But no! My consumption of Earth's resources is calculated at 1.2 earths. I am horrified. I think two major factors go against me: I drive a car and do not use public transport. There isn't any public transport in provincial New Zealand. Only cities get public transport. So surely the fact that I drive an electric car would swing the balance. Actually, the car has to be manufactured in the first place. Everything comprising it is mined or synthetic or rubber. So there's me. A 1.2 earth girl. I challenge you to take the test.

The Consumption Problem

Reducing consumption of all things is the first mechanism to employ in battling Earth overshoot. Congratulations for reading this book. You've taken the first step in wanting to make a change in your consumption habits. When you're done with it you can pass it on to be reused many times over. Reusing something is the second best thing we can do for the planet. It means energy is not spent on creating an item, thus fewer carbon emissions. And if you are worried about the social cost of less manufacturing, a market always finds its own level. People do find other jobs. Remember the days of privatisation and hundreds of job losses. People retrained or were absorbed into other industries or became owner operators. The new manufacturing is in green technology. People will and do find employment after the closure of traditional manufacturing plants.

Recycling is the third thing we can do to save the planet. In fact we must do it. When you purchase something you become responsible for the disposal of the packaging and for the ultimate disposal of the item. Take a good look at every component and be aware of its future disposal. Unfortunately not everything we consume is able to be recycled.

The world presently has a recycling crisis. China was the world's biggest receiver of recycling until January 2018 when it stopped taking other countries' rubbish citing that the population's health and safety was at risk because hazardous waste was often mixed in with the recyclables. New Zealand previously sold fifteen million tonnes of plastic per annum to China.[31] Countries across the world are now stockpiling twenty four types of waste plastic, glass and paper as they scramble to find a new market for it. Unfortunately Indonesia, Thailand and Malaysia have picked up some of this market, perhaps contaminating their own environment in their haste. This delays the producers facing the facts of the nasty consequences of their waste.

New Zealand presently ships recyclables to the above named countries although some waste is recycled locally. Unfortunately not all our waste is able to be sold and plastic is being dumped into landfills. Grades one, two and four plastics are grades New Zealand can recycle without too much trouble, but grades three, five, six and seven are more difficult.[32] Read the recycling labels. I see grade six on a lot of commercial packages. Leave what you can in the shop.

Not all waste is collected equally. Some countries collect recyclables already sorted into groups; that is, clean plastic of a certain grade in one group, glass sorted by colour. The countries doing this are able to continue to export waste to China. But many such as New Zealand collect all recyclables together which contaminates the whole lot. Those countries have been locked out of China.

Municipal authorities are now facing the problem of what to do with the piles of rubbish quickly accumulating in their cities. Some transport it to small towns where it is stockpiled or buried. The stockpiling of waste however, is a safety risk. A Thames facility has had two fires break out in as many years due to the storage of overheating lithium batteries. Toxic smoke filled the air as tonnes of plastic was incinerated.

Not every consumable is able to be recycled. Clean paper and cardboard are easy to recycle and mean fewer trees felled. However any products contaminated with grease or food cannot be recycled as grease from the food contaminates the clean paper. Paper napkins, paper towels and tissues are deemed too contaminated to recycle, and plastic coated cardboard that a lot of fast food comes in is not accepted for recycling. And if you think plain clean shredded paper gets the green light, think again. It clogs up the machines. There's one thing you can do with much of the above – put it in your compost.

Here is a list of paper based products that can't be recycled: laminated or foil coated wrapping paper, hardcover books, frozen food boxes, thermal fax paper, carbon paper, blueprints, aluminium foil boxes and binders.

Glass, aluminium and steel are also relatively easy to recycle. However, all glass is not created equal either. The following are unable to be recycled: window glass, pyrex baking dishes, light bulbs, fluorescent lights, mirrors, plate glass, eyeglasses and art glass.

Aerosols and spray bottles are something you should just stay away from. They will not recycle and of course nothing is going to eat them as they sit in a landfill. Picture the rows and rows of cleaning products and aerosols in the supermarket all proclaiming miraculous cleans. Now envisage all those bottles piled into a landfill. Luckily for the minimalist good old baking soda is a panacea for everything. You will never walk down that aisle again.

Plastics are a minefield. Not all plastics are created equal. Plastic bags are a single use item. They can't be recycled because they get caught in the machinery. Plastic bottle tops are grade five and cannot be recycled. This is why we are asked to remove the tops when we put plastic bottles in the recycling. Add to the list photographic film and microwave containers and you begin to realise how limited recycling plastic is. To that end we need to limit the purchasing of it in the first place.

New Zealand passed legislation banning single use plastic bags effective 2019. We can only hope that the demand for plastic bags of heavier grades does not increase. Critics say this is a drop in the ocean and will have no discernable effect on the problem of plastic in the environment. I say you have to start somewhere. People will think about the issue. Then hopefully they will begin to make a change in other facets of their lives for the good of the environment.

In summary here is a table of items that cannot be recycled:

1. Card or paper with food grease on it

2. Paper napkins, paper towels and tissues

3. Plastic coated cardboard

4. Shredded paper

5. Laminated or foil-coated wrapping paper

6. Hardcover books

7. Frozen food boxes

8. Thermal fax paper

9. Carbon paper

10. Blueprints

11. Aluminium foil boxes

12. Ring binders

13. Window glass

14. Pyrex baking dishes

15. Light bulbs

16. Fluorescent lights

17. Mirrors

18. Plate glass

19. Eyeglasses

20. Art glass

21. Aerosols

22. Spray bottles

23. Single use plastic bags

24. Plastic bottle tops

25. Photographic film

26. Microwave containers

Food Miles

A food mile is a factor taken into account when assessing the environmental impact of food. From the minute a crop is harvested until it reaches its destination on your dinner table it could have travelled a few kilometres or a few thousand kilometres. Transporting anything produces greenhouse gases in the form of carbon emissions. It would be lovely for us all to grow our own food but many people don't have space for a garden these days. And the ones that do would rather just buy fruit and vegetables, saving their scarce free time for other endeavours. In the space of approximately fifty years we've gone from just about everyone having a good-sized vegetable patch and a few fruit trees to having nothing. And while it can be argued that market gardens and commercial growers provide jobs, the growing of the crops and transporting the produce has a cost to the environment. It seems there are no free lunches. Someone or something always pays.

There are plenty of opportunities to buy locally. For instance, organic produce sold at a local farmer's market is likely going to outperform a similar product sold at the local supermarket. The vendor proudly stands by her produce and is able to tell you everything about it.

A supermarket chain usually belongs to one parent company that owns two or three supermarket chains across the price spectrum, that is, low prices, medium prices and high prices. They can do better in terms of food miles and fuel consumption per kilogram due to their bulk buying power. Added to the equation is the efficient agricultural techniques used on the farms contracted to those supermarkets.

But that isn't actually comparing apples with apples. For instance the supermarket produce is unlikely to be certified organic.

You can calculate food miles for certain foods using an online calculator. Its parameters are mileage and the carbon dioxide footprint. Find it here https://www.foodmiles.com.

Palm Oil

Palm oil is ubiquitous. It is found in baking and cleaning products, cosmetics and food. It has been around a long time, several kilograms having been found in Egyptian tombs dating to three thousand years Before Common Era. It was used alongside butterfat, olive oil, sunflower, safflower, cotton, grape, coconut and avocado oils as well as animal fats.

The industrial revolution triggered a demand for oil to make candles and lubricate machines. A palm oil supply was sourced from West Africa for these purposes but it wasn't until post World War I that technological improvements in refining edible oil allowed for the use of palm oil in food.[33]

Africa, Asia, North America and South America all grow Palm, elaeisguineensis (African), elaeis oleifera (American) and attaleamaripa. But they only account for fifteen percent of the world's entire production. Indonesia and Malaysia supply the rest. Eighty five percent of the world's production comes out of South East Asia.[33] This is a tragedy. This region of lush rainforests, like other tropical regions, hosts the highest biodiversity on the planet. This is an area where evolutionary change is relatively fast, where species are so specialised that they are adapted to incredibly tight geographical ranges. This is an area where our cousins, the orangutans, live along with sun bears, Sumatran tigers and rhinoceros. They can't just move on because we want to cut down their forests.

You can see that Indonesia and Malaysia are pretty special places because of the rainforest. But it is all under threat. The rainforest is being destroyed by fire to clear the land for palm crops. This habitat is home for some of the most threatened species on the planet, and is disappearing at the rate of fifteen hectares per hour.[34]

Let's put that in perspective. Fifteen hectares is equivalent to fifteen football fields or one hundred and eighty seven standard New Zealand house sites. That is a lot of streets of houses per hour razed to the ground. To really understand this I'm going to suggest something crazy. Imagine those houses are home to orangutans, sunbears, Sumatran tigers and rhinoceros. Because that is their home with special food they can't find anywhere else, they can't leave. They can't pack a suitcase of leaves and move across the river. They live where they live because of the food and that particular environment. They will die if they are forced to leave. Now it's clear how devastating this destruction is.

Quite frankly that is incredibly tough to get my head around. What it does reinforce to me though, is if I buy any product that has palm oil or kernel in it, then I have burnt down that forest and committed to death the beautiful animals that lived in the forest.

The consequences are sickening and not just for the immediate inhabitants of the rain forest. The release of carbon dioxide into the atmosphere is enormous. The air is constantly choked with particulates. Bad air leads to respiratory disease and early deaths of humans.

Orangutans, sun bears, rhinoceros and Sumatran tigers cannot survive this rate of destruction. And they won't. The World Wildlife Fund estimates that if nothing is done to curb this activity orangutans will become extinct in the wild within five to ten years and Sumatran tigers within three years. How dare we! How dare we force these animals to oblivion to satisfy our supposed need for palm oil/kernel.

Here's a concept that defies sense. Let's burn hectares and hectares of tropical rainforest – the most biodiverse land on planet earth, home to hundreds of thousands of species and plant a single crop: palm. And let's turn that palm oil into fuel. We could market it as biofuel, because hey, that's what it is. And people in rich countries can use it to fuel their cars so they can drive to the fast food outlet and buy a double beef burger.

Biofuel should be made from organic waste, not specially grown crops. I want to point out at this time, and I'm sure you've figured out by now, that palm crops are highly unlikely to be sustainable. It is an oxymoron. At some point rainforest was destroyed to make way for the crop. So these well intentioned but naïve sellers of homemade soap at local farmers' markets need educating if they tell you their palm oil is sustainable.

There is more devastation for the animals. New roads forged through the forest provide access for poachers that was never available in the past. So if the animals aren't burned to death they are caught and sold on the black market for the pet trade where they are kept in unconscionable conditions, or killed to make medicine and potions.

Marketers are becoming savvy to the buying public. They disguise the product under many different names. Apart from palm oil listed in the ingredients list you might look for these:

Lists such as this are freely available on the internet.

- PKO fractionations: Palm Kernel Stearin (PKs); Palm Kernel Olein (PKOo)

- PHPKO - Partially hydrogenated Palm Oil – where a liquid unsaturated fat is turned into a solid fat by adding hydrogen

- FP(K)O - Fractionated Palm Oil – higher concentration of saturated fat than regular palm oil

- OPKO - Organic Palm Kernel Oil

- Palmitate and any ingredient ending in palmitate - Vitamin A or Asorbyl Palmitate (NOTE: Vitamin A Palmitate is a very common ingredient in breakfast cereals. Vitamin A can be derived from vegetable oils)

- Palmate

- Sodium palmitate – the salts and esters of palmitic acid which is the major component of oil palms

- Sodium Laureth Sulphate (Can also be from coconut)

- Sodium Lauryl Sulphates (can also be from ricinus oil) – surfactant that causes foaming action

- Sodium Dodecyl Sulphate (SDS or NaDS) – the same as Sodium Lauryl Sulphate

- Sodium Lauryl Sulphate – (SLES) – synthetic detergent and surfactant used in personal care products, engine degreasers and floor cleaners. Surfactants make the bubbles.

- Sodium lauryl sulfoacetate (coconut and/or palm) – surfactant derived from palm and coconut oils. Skin friendly. Think of it as a detergent used in cosmetic products.

- ElaeisGuineensis – the name of the African palm oil, also called macaw fat

- Glyceryl Stearate – (GMS) – emulsifier in foods

- Stearic Acid – stear comes from the Greek word tallow. Saturated fatty acid obtained from fats and oils, typically palm oils

- Ethylhexyl palmitate or octyl palmitate – the fatty acid ester derived from 2-ethylhexanol and palmitic acid

- Steareth -20 – cleaning agent, surfactant and emulsifier used in skincare and personal care products. Synthetic compounds are created through the addition of stearyl alcohol, a fatty alcohol derived from stearic acid.

- Steareth -2 – as above but two units of ethylene oxide to one unit of stearyl alcohol

- Hydrated palm glycerides – the fatty acid component of palm oil. Hydrogenation allows the oily liquid to remain in a solid state at room temperature

- Sodium isostearoyllactylaye (derived from vegetable stearic acid) – food additive to improve mix and volume of processed foods (SSL label on food)

- Cetyl palmitate and octyl palmitate – derived from palmitic acid and cetyl alcohol. (names with palmitate at the end are usually derived from palm oil, but as in the case of Vitamin A Palmitate, very rarely a company will use a different vegetable oil)

- PKO - Palm Kernel Oil – This has many different names depending on how many carbons are in the chain. Many are used in the feedstock industry. Look for caproic, capric, caprilic, lauric, myristic, palmitic and stearic.

As minimalists who want to tread lightly on the planet we need to look for alternative natural products with which to clean the house and ourselves. Our best friend becomes baking soda, $NaHCO3$. From grubby surfaces in the kitchen to hair and teeth, baking soda is the must have product. But it does not substitute for soap.

Palm-oil free soap takes quite a bit of work to source. You will find that every bar of soap you pick up from the supermarket shelf has palm oil in it, even the eco-friendly looking soap. But all is not lost. There are companies specialising in the manufacture of palm oil-free soap and you just need to let your fingers do the walking. In New Zealand we have local companies making delicious natural soaps. Of course they are more expensive than the mass produced environmentally destructive products you are used to but as I have said before, admirable ethics deserve to be rewarded.

Carefully read the ingredient lists on biscuit packets, soap and other groceries. One form of protest against the use of palm oil is with your spending power. A twenty eight day challenge is offered on www.saynotopalmoil.com. The challenge is borne out of concern for the declining habitats of Sumatra and Borneo and the preservation of orangutans that make their home in those forests.

Plastic

Plastic is not as benign as it looks. It is made from hydrocarbons – that's oil, natural gas, coal, minerals and plants. Plastics comprise chains of hydrogen and carbon molecules linked together. A common term is polymers. Any word with the prefix poly in front means plastic. Do you have polypropylene clothes? That thermal underwear you paid through the nose for is actually carbon, hydrogen, oxygen, nitrogen, sulfur, chloride, fluoride and silicon. Maybe it is time to go back to one hundred percent wool for warm clothes.

Plastic contains bisphenol-A (BPA), 1,4 dioxane and alkylphenols. A colourless solid,bisphenol-A is soluble in organic solvents but poorly soluble in water. This product is ubiquitous. It is an endocrine disruptor. It can imitate the body's hormones, and it can interfere with the production, secretion, transport, action, function, and elimination of natural hormones. It can behave in a similar way to estrogen and other hormones in the human body. Note the products it is found in: plastic bottles, DVDs, CDs, epoxy resins in food tin coating, thermal paper used in till receipts, toiletries, feminine hygiene products, household electronics and sport equipment.[35] A test carried out in the United States found that of ninety five percent of adults tested by a urine test there were detectable levels of bisphenol. However another test identified bisphenol in sweat where it wasn't detected in urine.[36] This is worrying as bisphenol presence in laboratory animals affects reproductive systems.[37]

Plastics in the Ocean

Plastic waste is everywhere; from the highest slopes of the world's highest mountain, Mt Everest, Chomolungma, to the bottom of the deepest ocean trench on the planet, the eleven thousand metre deep Mariana Trench in Micronesia.Surely there can be no more compelling reason to become minimalist than this.

An incredible eight million tonnes of plastic is dumped into our oceans every year.[38] That is the equivalent of one truckload every single minute. And this is added to the one hundred and fifty million tonnes that are already in the oceans.But you don't see it bobbing around spoiling your view from your superyacht as seventy percent of marine debris sinks to the ocean floor.[39]

There are five giant plastic gyres in the world's largest oceans. A gyre is a great swirling vortex and these ones are comprised of rubbish. Circular ocean currents are created by the rotation of the planet. These currents move in a clockwise direction over some twenty million square kilometres and the circular motion draws debris into the stable centre where it becomes trapped.

The Great Pacific Garbage Patch is comprised of two gyres. The North Pacific Subtropical Gyre lies in a convergence zone between Hawaii and California and the Western Garbage Patch lies to the east of Japan. In March 2011 an earthquake struck Japan which resulted in a massive tsunami. That tsunami washed away an estimated 4.5 million tonnes of debris which travelled widely across the Pacific Ocean to the shores of western North America.[40] Different from the usual small debris washing around the oceans, the tsunami dislodged large items such as construction materials, ships and floating docks. Alarmingly, the total amount of debris created by that tsunami was ten times greater than the usual amount, or to put it another way, the amount was in the range of the global input of debris into the ocean each year and more than any other country other than China was estimated to produce in a whole year.[41]

Eighty percent of debris in these gyres derives from land-based activities in North America and Asia.[39] Rubbish from North America takes six years to reach the Great Pacific Garbage Patch whilst rubbish from Asia and Japan only takes one year.[39]

The South Pacific Gyre lies off the coast of Chile and Peru. An estimated seventy one thousand tonnes of plastic debris in the Pacific Gyres is from discarded fishing nets and this makes up the majority of the debris but there are also plastic chairs and shipping containers full of stuff that tipped overboard. The Pacific gyres cover approximately one million six hundred thousand square kilometres of ocean. In the centres of the gyres is where rubbish is thickest because it is trapped there. The density is shocking at approximately one hundred kilograms per square metre, fanning out to ten kilograms per square metre at the edges. It really is hard to imagine but most of the pieces of debris are smaller than a fingernail. The total weight is reportedly approximately eighty thousand tonnes.

The Atlantic Ocean has a gyre in the north which accumulates rubbish from the United States and Europe and a gyre situated off the coast of South America. The density of the debris in the North

Atlantic gyre is estimated to be two hundred thousand kilograms per square kilometre.

Of course the Indian Ocean does not escape. It too has a plastic-filled gyre swirling around. It was discovered in 2010 and only came to prominence whilst searching for the Malaysian jet ML370 in 2014. This gyre is situated between Australia and Africa and is approximately five million square kilometres. The debris circuits the entire ocean floating down the coast of Africa and over to Australia taking six years to complete the loop. An estimated rubbish density of ten thousand kilograms per square kilometre is swirling around the Indian Ocean.

These gyres cover such vast areas of the oceans they will be having an effect on the fish in those areas. Firstly, the soupy plastic upper column of water blocks the sunlight from hitting plankton and algae. Without sunlight they die. Fish and turtles that rely on plankton and algae for food starve. Then larger predators such as tuna, sharks and whales starve as the fish and turtles they feed on disappear. How many millions of humans rely on fish to survive?

Eventually the plastic sinks. It does not stay on or below the surface forever. It breaks down so small that it accumulates at the bottom of the world's deepest trenches.

A British research team captured amphipods, tiny crustaceans that resemble shrimps that feed off the seabed of these trenches, and found that eighty percent had either plastic fibres or plastic particles inside their guts. Further, they found that the deeper the trench, the higher percentage of plastic inside them. For example, in the Mariana Trench, the deepest underwater rift in the world, one hundred percent of the sea creatures surveyed had plastic in their guts. Of the six ocean trenches surveyed, including those from off the coasts of Japan, Chile and Peru, none had amphipods free of plastic inside them.[40]

At the surface of the gyres there is more plastic than natural predators which means that those fish which live near the surface are eating an awful lot of plastic. Surveys of sea turtles around the Great Pacific Garbage Patch have found that a staggering seventy four percent of the turtles' stomach contents contains plastic.[41]

Further, worldwide ninety one percent of turtles that become entangled in rubbish die, or are maimed, have limbs amputated or are choking. They cannot free themselves from the rubbish and are forced to drag it along with them. Loggerhead turtles mistake plastic bags for jellyfish which is a favourite food item. Imagine eating a plastic bag. What does that do to your insides? It would kill you. It kills turtles. Seals and other mammals drown in discarded nets. We even have a name for this: ghost fishing. Isn't it interesting that we have colloquialisms for practices we find distasteful.

It is not just sea creatures that mistake plastic rubbish for food. Seabirds are also vulnerable and it is believed that forty six percent of all seabirds eat plastic. That's the world's behemoth species such as albatross, molly mawks and petrels down to the smaller shearwaters, boobies, puffins, cormorants and gulls. Albatrosses mistake resin pellets for fish eggs and feed them to their chicks which of course die of starvation. I can't express how sad this makes me. You can't look at a seagull as you eat your fish and chips on the beach and know that it doesn't have plastic in its stomach. It probably does.

And that fish you're eating? It probably either ingested plastic directly or it ate a fish that had eaten plastic. As plastic breaks down it leaches bisphenol-A which is taken up by the fish as they eat the plastic. In addition plastic absorbs toxins from the environment so it is actually more toxic than when it entered the sea. The pollutants gather in the muscles of the fish and the toxins accumulate in larger amounts the further up the food chain they go.

You can see that plastic waste in the ocean has a knock on effect on humans. If you don't want to eat plastic, don't eat fish.

There is an effort underway at trying to clean up the largest of the ocean's plastic rubbish patches by using booms to scoop up debris. The problem is they can only scoop up so much rubbish and it has to be a certain size. Most plastic within the water column is so tiny it wouldn't be caught without sieving every living organism out of the sea. What the clean up does is prevent the disintegration of larger pieces of plastic into microscopic pieces. In essence there is only one way to stop rubbish accumulating in these gyres and that is to stop using and discarding plastic. With an estimated eight million tonnes of plastic entering the world's oceans each year it is a mammoth mission to change the practices of the last few generations but with a projection that by the year 2050 there will be more plastic waste in the sea than fish we must embrace environmentally sound practices.[42]

A Green Future

What does it mean to go green? Can we see a future where green jobs outnumber so called traditional jobs? The fact is there are trade-offs to be made. It is all very well to switch the entire world's vehicle fleet from fossil fuels to electric but all the components to manufacture the vehicles comes from the ground: metal is mined, plastic is made from hydrocarbons, tyres are made from rubber, the lithium for the battery is by the evaporation of highly concentrated lithium brine, as well as being mined. When it is laid out like that it seems we have a long way to go to achieve a sincerely green future.

Green jobs reduce the environmental impact of enterprises by improving the efficiency of energy and raw materials. The economy becomes decarbonised as greenhouse gases reduce and waste is minimised. Below is a list of green jobs that goes beyond most people' imagination of returning to market gardening.

- Environmental engineer

- Solar energy technician

- Recycling engineer

- Sustainable architect

- Solar energy systems engineer

- Solar panel technician

- Wind energy engineer

- Energy broker

- Securities and commodities broker

- Power plant operator

- Forest manager

- Insulation manufacturer

- Insulation installer

- Environment governance – local body

- Environment governance – central body

- Retrofitting green construction

- Research design consultation

- Green transport operator

- Service technician

At the moment green transport using electric vehicles is taking the world by storm. It feels like the car has been re-invented. The technology to improve battery efficiency is bolting ahead in leaps and bounds. And that's great for the planet right? These cars are powered by electricity and as long as the supply is sustainable there is no carbon dioxide hitting the atmosphere. Therefore the running of electric vehicles is clean and green.

But for every decision there is a consequence. And for purchasing an electric car it is this: lithium battery. The lithium for the battery is mined in the United States, Serbia, Australia, Canada, China and Mexico. Lithium extraction from evaporation ponds in Bolivia, Argentina, Chile and the United States however supply more lithium than from mining. Some say lithium extraction is dirty where toxic chemicals have leaked from evaporation ponds and infiltrated streams such as happened in Tibet. In Nevada effects from a processing plant killed fish one hundred and fifty miles downstream. Lessons must be learned from these episodes if lithium mining in Australia, Chile, China, Bolivia and Argentina is to be incident free. With an estimated twenty percent of all new vehicles to be new energy by 2020 it is inevitable there will be new mining.

Summary

Making minimal impact on the planet involves evaluating purchase decisions and being aware of alternatives. There will always be a trade-off because every action has consequences. For example, at the present time is the mining for lithium a lesser evil than burning fossil fuel? The topic deserves more space than I can devote to it but perhaps I've whet your appetite for research. We have a responsibility to inform ourselves on what is involved in getting our everyday products to market. If there is an aspect we don't like we can change our habits by voting with our money.

12

DE-CLUTTERING

"Live simply so that others may simply live." Ghandi (1869-1948)

At last we come to the business end. Hopefully after reading the above you will have gently conditioned your mind into the new way of approaching stuff. We're going to approach the *big de-clutter* systematically and methodically. Little by little we're going to work through one room at a time. That way it won't be overwhelming. I don't want you to cry out "I don't know where to start!"

Wardrobe

What better place to start than the smallest room in the house. I live in New Zealand and we have four seasons. Sometimes all seasons come in one day. I live in a one hundred year old wooden bungalow where not a lot of thought went into storage. But hey! What a blessing. Less storage equals less stuff. Net result where the wardrobe is concerned is that coats, jackets and winter gear gets hung in the garage during the summer and then a big switch around happens as the seasons change. I know that I'm lucky to have the garage but I also know that some of you have a wardrobe the size of a single garage. Lucky you. You can see all your clothes at one glance.

There are many approaches to the minimalist wardrobe, but the one constant is the amount of clothing. It is said that only twenty percent of clothes in our wardrobe actually get worn. The rest hang waiting for a special occasion, or for their owner to lose weight or to fall into favour again.

A minimalist must limit his or her wardrobe. It is impossible to see everything if there are three pieces on a hanger and difficult to make decisions if there is more than one of a style. That doesn't mean to say that pieces should be boring. They can, of course, be plain if that's your desire. There is a minimalist aesthetic that shuns frills, a simple silhouette being the aim. That's not me.

There is a 1970s idea called the capsule wardrobe. Kind of speaks for itself. I told you minimalism wasn't new. The idea is to have only a few items that stand the test of time. In a nutshell it saves you money and time and doesn't make you feel guilty.

Okay, let's get started minimalising that wardrobe. First you need to get yourself into the right mindset. No use starting this task if you're feeling tired or a little bit glum. It's something to look forward to. De-cluttering is a happy time. You've got to be happy to set your dresses free. So here we are, Saturday morning after a week at work. Forget about going to the market. Don't agree to breakfast with a friend. Tell her that today is minimising the wardrobe day and she's free to come over and bring a bagel. She might even leave with some clothes.

Drag everything out onto the bed. Everything! And while you're there you might as well vacuum the wardrobe and clean the shelves. You're going to have so few clothes (compared to before) that you're actually going to see the floor and the shelves. Now, how do the hangers look? Are they nice or are they crappy? You don't live with crappy anymore. It's all about quality. Throw them out. I mean, pass them on to the opportunity shop. However you might not want to replace them with plastic. Wood is good.

When I got serious about my wardrobe I decided to limit my palette. I have red hair and when I was a kid just about everything my parents made me wear was blue. I wasn't allowed to go near red, orange, yellow or pink. Anyway, in later years I discovered I could wear reds and oranges. So my wardrobe was a screaming mess. I thought about the practicalities of choosing three colours and my cleverest idea was to use green. There are about a zillion greens. My wardroom is green, black and cream. There is an accepted minimalist approach to fashion that advocates the dullest colours on the planet, like taupe! I can't imagine having a wardrobe full of taupe with only a necklace or brooch to tart it up. And I'm sure you can't either. Choose a colour palette and have fun with it. So there is a good place to start. Anything in the new colour palette stays. Put them back in your wardrobe.

Shopping for the new colour palette: This is incredibly fun and full of adventure. I have clothes in my collection that I would never have considered before. Some op-shop clothes are sorted by colour and it's so easy to quickly sort through the rack and find one piece. You don't have to actually wonder what it's going to go with, because it's going to go with everything. That's the beauty of the limited colour palette. Everything you buy is practically going to go with everything else. It is so easy to keep your money in your pocket. From time to time I have picked up a garment, remarked on its beauty or its quality and then mused "What a pity I don't wear red!" It is such a powerful anti-consumerist act.

There are some clever ideas around to help you determine when you last wore a garment like turning the hook of the hanger in the opposite direction after you've worn it. When you look at your hangers at the end of a season they would want to be all facing the same way. They won't be though. The idea is to discard the ones that face the original direction.

However, I find that tricks like that are merely a game. You know in your heart of hearts you didn't wear something in the last season. You really should pass it on. That's all you're doing. By donating to an op-shop you're doing a fine charitable act and giving someone else the chance to love the garment as much as you once did.

And if you've never worn it, well! Were you waiting for that special occasion? Or when you lost those love handles? Or perhaps you bought a dress for the ball and wore it once. Now it can go. It served its purpose. Next time there is a grand occasion such as a ball, visit the op-shop, pay $5.00 for something, even if you have to modify it. Who is going to know?

Now it's on to everything else. You just have to go through one by one and really analyse the garment. When did you last wear it? Does it fit? Does it need mending? If you haven't altered or mended a garment that is hanging in your wardrobe let's face it, you're never going to do it. Pass it on! There will be someone out there who it will fit.

Here's an interesting little adage you know to be true: "The more choice you have the harder it is to find something to wear." I once purchased a pack of three good quality shirts. I went halves with a friend. I ended up with two shirts. I could never decide which of the two shirts to wear and consequently didn't wear either of them. Only recently I passed one of them on to the op-shop. Now it's easy to wear the remaining shirt.

Once I had whittled my wardrobe down and was on the way to changing my clothes over to the new palette I made a rule: one comes in – one goes out. So if I add a shirt something has to make way for it. Over time you'll find your whole wardrobe has transformed, hopefully sourced from op-shops, for that really is a fair way for goods to recycle and support your favourite charity at the same time. Incidentally, I donate to one charity, the SPCA, but I do buy from all the op-shops. I don't want to feel guilty about not giving to them all fairly. There are seven of them in my small town, so to keep things simple I only donate to my favourite. Keeps life really clean.

Of course now there is the underwear drawer. That shouldn't be so hard to skinny down, surely. Just think if you were hit by a bus and had to go to hospital! Out go the grandma's baggy britches please. There is no loose elastic in your house.

And I'll bet you didn't know you owned that many socks. Actually socks can be useful when you apply the one in, one out rule. Sometimes I've really struggled to find something to throw out but then I find a pair of socks with loose tops. Bingo!

The wardrobe is something a minimalist needs to keep vigilant about. Stuff can sneak in, like a belt that came with a dress when the dress actually got passed on. So it's beneficial to have a cull every

194

couple of months. It will amaze you but there is always something that has to leave.

A new wardrobe is a good way to practice social and environmental conscience. I now only buy second hand clothes made of one hundred percent cotton, silk, linen, hemp, cashmere or wool. If you regularly browse opportunity shops you will find these treasures. It is also an easy way to keep money in my pocket because I am not buying clothes just because they are the right colour.

Shoes

"The more you have the more you are occupied. The less you have the more free you are." Mother Theresa

I've never been big on shoes but over the last few years my rule has been this: one new pair of boots for winter – and to be fair they last a few years so I have quite a few pairs - and one pair of shoes for summer. These are my every day work shoes. I buy these in October and throw them out in April, having worn them every day. For in between seasons I have a couple of pairs. For me there are trainers, cycling and tramping boots and only one strappy black pair which would be about ten years old and come out less than once a year. I just don't see how a person could accumulate fifty pairs or more. A minimalist wouldn't want to. My pocket is better off.

Lounge

"Maintaining an extravagant lifestyle tends to outweigh the pleasure of partaking in it." Epicurus (341-270 BC) Greek philosopher

Stand in the middle of your lounge if you don't mind. Do you know where to start? No? The goal of minimalism is to enjoy the space. A clear surface is a beautiful thing. A shelf with one object is a beautiful thing. A mantlepiece full of dust collectors is a nightmare.

Let's start with the mantlepiece. Take everything off it. Polish the mantelpiece. Choose one piece. Polish it. Place it in the centre of the mantelpiece. Analyse the remaining pieces. There are lots of questions here. Can you discard any then and there? And by discard I always mean pass on to someone else to enjoy via an op-shop. Great if you can. Grab a box and start filling.

It's probably a bit tougher than that isn't it? I have antiques from both my grandmothers. My problem is that I love these ornaments. My way around the knick knack conundrum is this: I chose twelve special pieces, eleven of which I keep in my antique tall boy. On the first day of each month I place a different ornament on the mantelpiece. Thus, one ornament commands the room. I love the first day of the month. The biggest decision is choosing which ornament for that month. You don't know how exciting that is!

You will find that over time you will be able to discard most of your dust collectors. I could say you should list things for sale on Trademe or Buy Sell Trade but in my experience it's certainly not worth the effort. Far easier to donate to the op-shop and it's done. With antiques however, you can sell to the antique dealer. At least it's something. And here's a thought to ponder. In actual fact your goods are worth virtually nothing when you come to sell them so if you desperately miss something you can always buy them back for next to nothing. But I'll bet you don't miss anything and you'll be so far along the minimalist journey you wouldn't dare to contemplate it.

Let's look at the bookcase. If you're reading this book on an e-reader, congratulations. You're already well on the way to becoming a minimalist. An e-reader can contain hundreds of books. If you spent $6 or $7 on a good book at a book exchange consider this: you swapped a book. You're not even going to keep it! Spend the same on an e-book and you get to keep the book plus the pages haven't been turned by someone else's filthy fingers. And because you get to keep the e-book you can return to it, reference it and read it again, as many times as you like. And here's where it gets really exciting if you are travelling. You can download an e-reader app onto your phone and download your favourite books. This is amazing. I can read my books anywhere I please. Also, on the phone app the covers are in colour which is exciting since my e-reader is the most basic model and only does black and white. Above all, e-readers do not utilise paper, which has to be a good thing.

You don't need to worry about the written word disappearing just because you've gone electronic. The written word is a highly compressed, coded form of the spoken word. [1] There is great skill in writing. And, we can read a great deal faster than someone reading the same text.

As a minimalist you want to pass on your books. It's hard. You have a love affair with books. You paid good money for them, they are part of a set, they look lovely on the shelf, all those spines lined up like fence palings. It's incredibly hard to set them free. But you have to. I bet you didn't actually read them twice anyway. Let someone else enjoy them.

I acknowledge that text books and coffee table books occupy a special place. There will come a time in every minimalists life that they will ask "Do I really need all those texts from university?" Need? Huh! Did you even refer to them when you started your career? No. They are sitting on a shelf or in a box simply to remind you of those wonderful days of learning and new friends. But you have moved on. They need to go.

Look at your walls. What's wrong with them? How do they make you feel? Minimalism demands space. It is a vital part of the lifestyle. Remember space is more important than the object. The object can only be fully appreciated if it is not competing with other objects. It demands that your eye be drawn to it and then focused on it to the exclusion of everything else in the room.

Many people hang dozens of family photos of family members on the walls. It's embarrassing for those poor people in the photos and it gives an enormous sense of clutter to a room. If you're going to hang portraits, squish them together so it creates a montage. Then allow a lot of space between that collection of photos and the next set.

The room should balance. Stand in the centre of the room and close your eyes. Imagine the space with the walls as they are, perhaps cluttered, perhaps empty. Do you feel heavy towards the full wall and lighter towards the empty wall? Now try to balance the space. Remember how those minimalist architects achieved less is more by skilfully using voids? You want to feel calm within the space.

Now we will move onto the furniture. A clear table is a beautiful thing. Feel its surface, smell the polish. A table is not home to a collection of papers that you don't quite know what to do with. You don't want the remotes, the tv guide or last month's *Listener* cluttering its surface. Let the table be there for you when you want it, for example to place your cup of tea on. Don't treat it like a permanent storage shelf.

How's the lounge suite, the lamps, the tiny corner table? Regard these as art works in their own right. Isn't this what the Bauhaus strived for? Sure, they are items of utility, but when you remove clutter from the room they hold court. Your eye will assess them differently. Remember that space is your friend. If your rooms feels cluttered from the amount of furniture then I'm afraid you will just have to let some of it go.

For each piece of furniture stand back and say to yourself "Is that the best I can display it? Does it show it off to its best?"

There is a very good reason to keep the lounge clear of clutter. In winter some of us are still lucky enough to have a fire. As wonderful as this is the fire always wafts a thin veneer of white dust over everything. Long before I became a minimalist I used to pack up my dust collectors off the mantelpiece into a box for the winter. One year I didn't put them back!

There is another reason to fully appreciate the couch or the table – someone made it. Resources were mined, extracted, harvested and made usable. Buildings were constructed to house a furniture factory. People were employed to design and manufacture the furniture. Their wages provided food and shelter for their families. The couch or the table is not worth nothing. It doesn't deserve to be hidden under great piles of papers and clutter. Give it space. Honour it.

Kitchen

I'll bet you can stand in your kitchen and say you need everything in it. That's understandable because I'm sure nearly everything is in cupboards and drawers. But look harder. First of all, are there things in here that don't belong in the kitchen? Do you have a bowl for keys or business cards? Or your wallet or phone? Uh-uh. No way Jose. They have to move. The kitchen is the business end of the house. Remember what we said about clear surfaces? This is doubly important in the kitchen, obviously, for hygiene reasons.

I think a terrific place to start minimalising is the fridge. Get rid of those fridge magnets. How can you clean that beautiful white door with all that clutter stuck to it. Why not just pick say two of your favourites and stick them to the side of the fridge where you don't notice them. Then you can use them if you really need to stick a note on the door. Now just so you feel really good about this you can wash and polish your fridge door. Yes I said polish. No one said polish was only for the lounge. Already you've minimalised and created a beautiful clear surface.

For some reason most of us like to have enough crockery, cutlery and glasses to host a street party. When did that last happen? Ever? We've all gained bits and bobs of kitchen paraphernalia and we've all lost some. You will want to be able to retrieve what you use every day without having to move six things to get to it. In my house we've had two pots for as long as I can remember. We had a go at having three pots and it felt decadent. In the end something happened to pot number three and we were relieved to return to being a two pot household. How often do you use all your pots at once anyway? I'll bet it's never. This should tell you that you don't want any more pots than you have elements on the stove.

How easy is it to access your pots? Unless you have a modern house with one of those pull-out pot drawers, the answer is not easy. If you use a pot every day put it on the top shelf in the cupboard. For some reason pots get relegated to the bottom shelf but you don't really want to bend all the way down there unless you've set yourself some exercise regime.

You can look at how many people there are in your household and skinny down your kitchen clutter accordingly. Unfortunately when there is a husband involved the amount you can get rid of (for example cups) without starting World War III can be limited. But you can de-clutter areas that husbands don't go to like the baking tray department. I make no apology for my sexist terminology for in my house this is my experience.

Kitchen gadgets are a minimalist's nightmare. You hardly use them and they take up space. More often than not they break down to fifty nine pieces and are a curse to wash and dry. Just think, your grandmother used a knife for everything and at the end of the day she only had a knife to wash, and a knife to leave for your inheritance. Wonderful. Today we've got apple corers, cherry stoners, nut crackers, rice cookers, mandolins, zucchini spirallers, ice cream scoops. The list goes on and on. There are shopping channels on television dedicated to selling junk gadgets. Let's stop the madness. All I need is a small blender and a set of good knives. I reckon you could dispense with fifty percent of what's in your kitchen cupboards.

Have you thought about cookbooks? I used to have a cupboard full of them. Now I've skinnied it down to eight, five of which are vegan and two of which are my own vegan folders, one for savoury and one for sweet. The other is my indispensible soup book. Thanks to the internet we don't really need to cram our cupboards full of cookbooks. I go online to find what I want. It frees up my cupboards for more important things, like food!

All kitchens have cupboards no one can reach. Mine go all the way up to my ceiling and I have a ten foot stud which means I have to be eight foot tall to see inside them. Over the years I used to keep stuff up there which meant it was always a surprise to see that stuff again, since I never actually went up there. It wasn't until I became a minimalist that I realised I didn't need that stuff. I had simply housed it because I could. I am proud to say that those ridiculously high cupboards are now empty.

You may not have cupboards as high as those but you will have a corner cupboard. Get down on your knees and drag everything out. If you haven't used something or even seen it for a while, now might be the time to set it free.

Linen Cupboard

Is yours one of those cupboards that you have to hold the towels with one hand while you quickly slam the door with the other? This is an area where stuff sneaks up. You need to pull everything out and dump it on the floor into piles: sheets, pillow slips, towels, hand towels, flannels, embroidered cloths if you're lucky enough to have those and blankets. Areas you need to address are the following:

The state of the item: Frayed edges, thin, worn or moth eaten? Excellent. You don't need to think about this. Chuck it out. These can go into the discard pile immediately. Don't be embarrassed. The SPCA want these items so they can be the first things to set free.

The number of beds in the house: You need two sets of sheets and pillowslips per bed. That's one set on the bed and one set in the wash or the linen cupboard at any given time. Trust me, you do not need a whole shelf crammed full of linen if you only have three beds.

The number of people living in the house: Same deal. Two towels, two flannels and two handtowels per person. That's one towel in use and the other in the wash or beautifully folded on the shelf.

The next items can be tricky since it's highly likely that hand embroidered cloths, table cloths and woollen blankets have been passed down by a significant family member. Firstly you can scope out other family members to see if they'd like them. Don't make assumptions that they'll say no. Explain your mission and you may be surprised by the answer. If this doesn't work pick out the ones you really can't part with, fold them and place them on a now spacious shelf in the linen cupboard. These need to be eye level. You probably couldn't even see these items before but now they are going to be right in your face every time you open the door. This is great. Soon you will realise that these things will have to be let go, unless of course you start using them. What is really comforting is that when you take these items to an op-shop you're giving someone the chance to love them more than you do and you're doing your charity a service. Good on you.

Bathroom

This is one of the easiest rooms to de-clutter. There are unlikely to be antiques or items for which you are emotionally attached to.

The vanity top should be clear of anything you don't use every day. Toothbrushes, toothpaste, creams and potions can be kept very tidy in an attractive bowl. This gives the impression the bench is clear because there is only one thing on the bench. So there you have it – soap and a bowl. Vanity top done.

Now it's time to look inside the cupboards. There will be potions, pills and medicines long past their expiry date. Get rid of this junk. This has to be the easiest de-cluttering you will do.

Towels. I live in a two person household and we host touring cyclists so I don't have many towels. Eight. Remember, one in use and one up your sleeve per person. I keep all the towels in the bathroom. They are either in use or stored on the shelf. Same goes for flannels and handtowels. This frees up space in the linen cupboard for bed linen and table cloths.

Here's some motivation for you. If you can't choose which towels to keep and which to ditch, set the whole lot free and treat yourself to a whole new matching set.

Remember the SPCA needs towels so your threadbare or raggedy towels can most definitely have a second life.

Those boxes in the bottom of the wardrobe

Or the top of the wardrobe, or the attic or the garage. You know the ones I mean. The contents of these will include every university assignment you ever wrote, photos so old the colours are faded and you can't tell who is in them because the people are orange, your favourite toys, old postcards, your grandmother's tea set.

This is the tough stuff. These are the things you keep because you think you'll feel guilty if you throw them away. But you don't know that because you haven't set any of it free.

Start with the items that weren't someone else's. Say, toys. Why are you keeping them? Are they a thread to your childhood? Do you think your childhood memories are going to disappear just because you set free a tin soldier? Of course they aren't. If you think something has antique quality try listing it on Trademe or take it to your local antique dealer. Chances are it is worth close to nothing. Does that speak to you? You've been let down with a thump. This should tell you that your attachment to the item is strongly emotional. Still having trouble setting it free? Okay, look, if you don't pass it on now, it will probably be the first thing your children dump when you're dead and left the house full of clutter. The great thing about tackling the issue now is that you are in control. You can choose which charity to give it to. Someone else will buy it and love it. It will have a second chance. You really need to think about these items as being set free.

Another reason you're hanging onto toys may be that you want your grandchildren to play with them. Let's just analyse that. You have a romantic idea that the grandchildren you don't yet have will want to play with toys that your own children played with. It's a long shot at best. I say do yourself a favour and pass them on. Let the future take care of itself.

Photos. This is a great one. Remember all those seventies Kodak prints stuck and I really mean stuck, inside those big old albums with a sheet of plastic over them. You don't have to say goodbye to these. However, it does take a lot of work.

One by one disassemble each album and decide which pages to scan. All these memories can be saved digitally and catalogued onto your computer. How clever is that? Now the bulky boxes of decades old photos can go in the rubbish. There may be family members who would appreciate the hard copies and you could ask them if they'd like them. Don't forget to back up onto a memory stick. Chances are you haven't even looked at those photos for ten years and of course there's no guarantee you'll ever look at them again. But you've dealt with a massive emotional problem and you still have the photos. Genius.

This is a big job and it's a great winter job; just you and your computer while it's rainy and cold outside. It's actually great fun going through the photos and letting the memories take over for a while.There probably will be photos of family members that have been passed down to you. I urge you to scan these then try really hard to find family members to pass them onto. They'll get them when you die, right? Make it someone else's problem for now.

Home Office

It's a paper war. The first place to start is to limit the amount of paper that comes into the house. Choose to receive your bills by email. Then when they arrive you simply save them into an electronic folder. For example under Documents you want to click New Folder then rename it Electricity. Go into that folder and click New Folder again. Now name it the current year. Eventually you could have many folders organised in the main folder called electricity. You can keep going with your new folders within folders for as many categories as you need. For example, under Electricity<2018 you may need "weekly usage" plus "monthly invoice". So you get 52 weekly reports and twelve month invoices all neatly filed in 2018. And not a single piece of paper takes up space on your desk.

Continue in this manner for as many creditors that will send their invoices online. For those that don't, plus things like property valuations, statements, car repairs, simply scan the document, file electronically then recycle the hard copy.

You have now become paperless. It's a big task to implement but when you have it up and running it's quick to maintain and you never have a build up of piles of paper. It has the added advantage of this: when you sit there for two minutes scanning and filing you tend to read the document. Before I went paperless I tended to quickly plonk the paper on the pile intending to read it later. That never happened.

There will be some documents you shouldn't discard to make life easier later on. For example, anything you might need to give to the accountant or that might support your end of year tax. Whilst you have it digitally and are able to print it out, it's just as easy to keep them in a box for that express purpose.

I used to give piles of supporting documents to my accountant each year until he lost a whole lot. If I had been paperless at that time I could easily have printed off the required documents, or better yet given him the memory stick and told him to find them himself, or when I had calmed down, simply emailed the required folders. So there is a good reason to adopt the paperless approach.

De-cluttering can become addictive. It's like a runner's high. There is a euphoric feeling about the process and its pleasing result. The home can be the one place in this frenetic world that you have control. Exercise it.

13

CONTINUING THE PRACTICE

"Poverty is my pride." Muhammed

When you can say to yourself "I am a minimalist" purchasing decisions are taken out of your hands. For example, a crock pot in the appliance store looks nice. It's a sleeker design than the one you presently have. Before you became minimalist you might well have bought it and passed the old one along. But now it holds no attraction for you. It goes against everything you believe to flippantly exchange one perfectly good functional crock pot for a newer one. In fact you can walk throughout the store – if for some strange reason you happen to be in an appliance store in the first place – and feel impervious to all that glittering advertising and feel ill at the waste of power that all the televisions are sucking up. You actually feel that you are above all this. Other people are beguiled by this rampant consumerist society. Not you. You ARE a minimalist. And as such you don't have to make decisions or justify your non-expenditure.

There are some tools to help you stick to your resolve. If you are not sure why you buy stuff you might find the financial tools work for you. Everyone has a trigger and it's just a case of finding it. Perhaps you mix with people who put too much emphasis on the things they own and without realising it, you buy stuff to impress them.

Here is one financial tool to help you become a better minimalist. You've heard of this and it isn't new and it isn't sexy. It's called budgeting.

Accounting for every dollar is one way to curb your spending habits. I will bet you don't have a budget worksheet. How much money do you spend each week on stuff other than household expenses? How much money do you spend each week? If you were to record every dollar you spend for one week you would be shocked. If you don't know where your money goes then you are out of control. It is a powerful feeling to be in control of your spending.

Budget worksheets are available online so I'm not going to provide one but I am going to explain how they work. You could even just make one up yourself it is so easy, but the fun thing about it is that you do not need to think too hard because all the calculations are done for you and if you change one figure the totals are changed automatically.

It is all about money coming in and money going out. The income is the short column. Put everything in there: wages, bonuses, rents received.

Now think about your weekly spend. These will be items such as groceries, petrol, Friday lunch. This is one group of expenses. Total them.

The next group is monthly payments. Put utilities in here and expenses that are paid monthly. Make a column next to the first column. This is for the calculation of the monthly amount to a weekly figure. If you are doing this manually you need to multiply the monthly figure by twelve to get the amount for the entire year, then divide by fifty two weeks. You need to do this because some months have four weeks and some have five.

The third block of payments is for annual expenses like insurances on vehicles, house and contents, AA subscription. If you pay these monthly make a note about that. Don't forget to add your savings. Now make a weekly amount column next to that column.

There will now be three totals in the expenses columns. Add the three weekly expense columns and subtract that total from the weekly income. This will hopefully show a surplus. Now you can see how much money you really do have to spend. It's likely you could afford to put more money into savings instead of frittering it away every week on the latest sale items.

If making a budget excites you, the next step is to draw up a cash flow. This is where you list all your regular income expenses down the left hand column. Just use the same items from the budget worksheet. Next write the dates one week apart at the top of the spreadsheet. Find the dates that fit bill payments and write the amount of the bill in the box. For example, the power bill is paid monthly by direct debit on the twentieth day of each month. Look along the columns to find which week the twentieth will fall and write the dollar amount for the power. You can do this for six months or twelve months out.

What do you think is going to happen if you fill out all the expenses and you operate on a surplus? The surplus amount each week gets added to the income section. Very quickly it becomes obvious that a nice nest egg will accumulate if you are sensible with your spending and you stick to your budget.

It can be helpful to do the above exercises if you have a specific goal. Make the goal achievable. Don't aim so high you're going to beat yourself up when you can't achieve it. This is about empowerment. A budget worksheet and a cash flow are extremely powerful tools. By taking the time to draw them up in the first place shows a willingness to take control. Your commitment to reduced spending might still need some work however.

A couple of things can help. If you purchase goods with cash chances are you won't want to buy anything. We still don't associate a plastic card with money even though they have been around for forty years.

You could set yourself a mini challenge. For example don't shop for pleasure for one week, or two weeks or more. This will be easier if you have created a budget worksheet and a cash flow. You won't want to muck those up.

Remember that you are an individual. Don't compare yourself to other people. What makes them happy isn't going to make you happy.

And you don't need to buy something to impress friends. That would be pretty shallow wouldn't it? On your part and theirs. Besides, how do you know they can really afford the latest gadgets that you see them with? They may have used credit cards, inheritance money or lotto winnings. Don't let it bother you. Be true to yourself.

There are more beautiful things you can do with your time than shop for pleasure. Go for a walk, do yoga, meditate, play sport. These are activities that involve the act of being present.

But buying things makes us feel good. It shows we have control over something, in this case, that we have made a decision. Retail therapy does exist. Buying on a whim makes us feel terrific. But there is also buyer's remorse. In the cold light of day the reality of what we've bought or signed up to dawns on us and we realise we can't afford it. So why did we buy it in the first place? Because it was presented in such a way that we felt great. We picked it up, stroked it, imagined it in our house. In our minds we had to have it. Shouldn't have touched it. Gave us feelings of ownership.

Fortunately our social watchdogs recognise this trap. For people who have signed up to something with payments to be made over time, there is what is called a cooling off period. In the teeny tiny fine print there is a clause giving us seven days to cancel the contract. Unfortunately most people will wait until the first couple of payments go out of their pay to realise the decision was not a wise one and they can't actually afford it. Oh for the budget worksheet! Using the budget worksheet as an excuse not to spend can take pressure off. It's not me that can't afford it! The budget says I can't. "That's not in the budget" is a very powerful statement.

I have placed emphasis on the need to be environmentally responsible when purchasing stuff. There is a superior feeling in knowing that you are living lighter on the planet than you used to be. It is not too late to start treading lightly. We did not consciously set out to buy unethical or unsustainable products. It is only with hindsight that we have become aware of the high cost to the planet of our decadent lifestyle. We now know that we cannot continue to live the life we were living. The future of our planet depends on us changing the way we purchase goods.

Tell people you are minimising. It is easier to be true to your goal when you hear it out loud. Friends may come on board. In fact you really want them to help, especially cleaning out the kitchen, the linen cupboard and your wardrobe. Why not announce a pre-opportunity shop scavenge and get your friends around to unload some stuff. This is a sure-fire way of reducing your trips to the opportunity shop.

Very soon you will be telling people "I'm a minimalist." Say it to yourself enough times and believe it. Here are some practical steps you can take:

- Draw up a budget worksheet

- Draw up a cash flow chart

- Use the affirmation "I am a minimalist"

- Use cash to purchase goods

- Don't let stuff into your home without releasing other stuff

References

Chapter 2

1. Barry Schwartz, The Paradox of Choice, TED Global, 2005

2. https://www.changingminds.org

Chapter 5

1. NZ Herald Business 17/4/18

2. https://www.economist.com 7 September 2017

3. https://www.economist.com 7 September 2017

4. International Labour Organisation

Chapter 6

1. Modern Art Insight, Movements, Styles and Tendencies, https://www.theartstory.org

Photo credits

2. Malevich's Suprematism Supremus No. 56, 1916. Image retrieved from Wikimedia Commons. Public Domain.

3. Malevich's Black Square, 1915. Image retrieved from Wikimedia Commons. Public Domain.

4. Malevich's White Square on White, 1917. Image retrieved from Wikimedia Commons. Public Domain.

5. Mondrian's Composition with Red, Yellow, Blue and Black, 1921. Image retrieved from Wikimedia Commons. Public Domain.

Chapter 8

Photo credits

1. Ando's Row House or Azuma House. Image retrieved from Wikimedia Commons. Author Oiuysdfg. Creative Commons Attribution-share Alike 3.0 Unported. No changes were made.

2. The Rietveld Schroder House. Image retrieved from Wikimedia Commons. Available under license: Creative Commons Attribution-share Alike 3.0 Unported. No changes were made.

3. Rietveld's Red Blue Chair. Image retrieved from Wikimedia Commons. Author Sailko. Available under license: Creative Commons Attribution-share Alike 3.0 Unported. No changes were made.

4. Gropius's Bauhaus, 1929. Image retrieved from Wikimedia Commons. Author Lannguyen138. Available under license: Creative Commons Attribution-share Alike 4.0 International. No changes were made.

5. Gropius's Bauhaus, 1929. Image retrieved from Wikimedia Commons. Author M_H.DE. Available under license: Creative Commons Attribution-share Alike 3.0 Unported. No changes were made.

6. Le Corbusier's L'Espirit Nouveau Pavilion, 1925. Image retrieved from Wikimedia Commons. Author SiefkinDR Available under license: Creative Commons Attribution-Share Alike 4.0 International. No changes were made.

7. Le Corbusier's 1929 Villa Savoye. Image retrieved from flickr user YoGomi. Available under license: Attribution-ShareAlike 2.0 Generic (CC BY-SA 2.0)https://creativecommons.org/licenses/by-sa/2.0/. No changes were made.

8. Oud's Weissenhof Estate apartments, 1927. Photo shows the back of the apartments. Image retrieved from Wikimedia Commons. Author Andreas Praefcke. Available under license: Creative Commons Attribution 3.0 Unported. No changes were made.

9. Mies' German Pavilion for the 1929 Barcelona Exhibition. Image retrieved from Wikimedia Commons. Author "© Alice Wiegand / CC BY-SA 3.0 (via Wikimedia Commons)". License created under: Creative Commons attribution-Share Alike 3.0 Unported. No changes were made.

10. Mies' Tugendhat House in Czech Republic, 1930. Rear view. Image retrieved from Wikimedia Commons. Author Daniel Fišer (-df-). Available under license: Creative Commons Attribution-Share Alike 3.0 Unported. No changes were made.

11. Mies' Tugendhat House. Upper level. Image retrieved from Wikimedia Commons. Author Rory Hyde. Available under license: Creative Commons Attribution-Share Alike 2.0 Generic

12. Gropius House, 1938, Massachusetts. Image retrieved from Wikimedia Commons. Author Daderot. Available under licence: Creative Commons Attribution-Share Alike 3.0 Unported. No changes were made.

13. Gropius House, Massachusetts. Side view. Image retrieved from Wikimedia Commons. Author Magicpiano. Available under license: Creative Commons Attribution-Share Alike 3.0 Unported. No changes were made.

14. Johnson's Glass House 1947-1949, New Canaan, Connecticut. Image retrieved from Wikimedia Commons. Author Edelteil. Available under license: Creative Commons Attribution-Share Alike 3.0 Unported. No changes were made.

15. The guest house on the grounds of Johnson's Glass House. Image retrieved from Wikimedia Commons. Author Staib. Available under license: Creative Commons Attribution-Share Alike 3.0 Unported. No changes were made.

16. Mies' SR Crown Hall, 1950-1956 at the Illinois Institute of Technology in Chicago. Image retrieved from Wikimedia Commons. Author Joe Ravi. Available under license: Creative Commons Attribution-Share Alike 3.0 UnportedCC-BY-SA 3.0. No changes were made.

17. Mies' Seagram Building, 1958, New York. Imaged retrieved from Wikimedia Commons. Author Max Hermus. Public domain.

Chapter 9

1. Adam Dudding, Sunday Star Times, www.bosarchitecture.co.nz

2. Massey University Affordability Index

3. The Cost of Building in New Zealand

4. Quotable Value, Retrieved from www.qv.co.nz

5. New Zealand Herald, Statistics New Zealand

6. htpp://www.level.org.nz

Chapter 10

1. Retrieved from http://www.newgeography.com, 11 April 2017

2. Food and Agriculture Organisation of the United Nations, www.investopedia.com 25 June 2019

3. Retrieved from http://www.publicinternational.org and http://www.animalethics.org.uk

4. Stuff, 25 July 2018, Lynley Tulloch

5. Pork Industry Board

6. App.com, Part of USA Today Network, 17 July 2016

7. The Conservation. Xenotransplantation: using pigs as organ and tissue donors for humans. Peter Cowan. 14 December 2011.

8. Retrieved from www.nzpork.co.nz

9. SAFE, Pat Deavoll, 29 October 2018

10. New Zealand Poultry Association.

11. Stuff, 7 October 2016

12. https://www.mpi.govt.nz/dmsdocument/1441-meat-chickens-animal-welfare-code-of-welfare-2012

13. Egg Producers Federation of New Zealand

14. http://www.worldpopulationreview.com/continents/world-population/

15. http://www.worldatlas.com

16. New Zealand Dairy

17. Statistics New Zealand

18. Retrieved from http://www.bbc.com/howfertilizerhelpedfeedtheworld/Tim Harford, 2 January 2017

19. Food and Agriculture of the Organisation of the United Nations, Fertilizer Outlook Expert Group, June 2016

20. Retrieved from www.large.stanford.ed, "The Fertilizer Industry, World Food Supplies and the Environment," International Fertilizer Industry Association, December 1998. S. Wood and A. Cowie, "A

Review of Greenhouse Gas Emission Factors for Fertiliser Production," IEA Bioenergy, June 2004.

21. Food and Agriculture of the Organisation of the United Nations

22. Retrieved from http://www.timeforchange.org

23. American Museum of Natural History, retrieved from http://www.sciencedaily.com, 2 December 2016

24. Food and Agriculture of the Organisation of the United Nations

25. United Nations Development of Economic and Social Affairs

26. Listener, 21 May 2016

27. http://www.bodybuzz.co.nz

28. Medical News Today, 15 November 2017, 1984 Michigan State University Report on vegetarian versus meat eaters and bone density

29. Max Roser (2018), "Life Expectancy", Published online at http://www.ourworld.oeg/life-expectancy

30. http::://www.vegansociety.com

Chapter 11

1. Ministry for the Environment

2. Recycle New Zealand

3. https://www.CO2.earth

4. Landcare Research

5. Agency for Toxic Substances and Disease Research. Landfill Gas Primer. Retrieved from https://www.atsdr.cdc.gov

6. Ministry for the Environment

7. Ministry for the Environment

8. Avfall Sverige Report, Patrick J Kiger, https://www.science.howstuffworks, 9 July 2018

9. Mother Nature Network. https://www.volund.dk

10. NASA Earth Observatory

11. CO2 Earth Home Page

12. Science News, Vol. 192, No. 10, December 9 2014, p124

13. NASA Earth Observatory

14. NASA Earth Observatory

15. Centre for Climate and Energy Solutions, http://www.gfkl.noaa.gov; 6 June 2018

16. World Atlas

17. Sapiens: A Brief History, YN Harari

18. Drew McFarlane, The Weather Channel, 1 March 2019

19. National Geographic. United Nations Intergovernmental Panel on Climate Change, 2 February 2014

20. "Ludwig-Maximilians-Universtat Munchen. Five new frog species from Madagascar." Science Daily, 28 March 2019

21. BBC.com from Sydney Morning Herald, 20 February 2019

22. World Wildlife Fund, Living Planet Report 2016

23. Pacific Marine Environmental Laboratory

24. Jo Chandler, Yale Environment 360, 31 March 2014; https://www.ncel.net//oceanacidification

25. https://www.sciencemag.org, Reef Resilience Network. Wilkinson, C (ed.), 2004. Status of Coral Reefs of the World. 2004. Vol.1 Australian Institute of Marine Science, Townsville, Queensland, Australia, 301p.

26. Food and Agriculture Organisation of the United Nations, Global Forest Resources Assessment 2015, 2nd Edition

27. World Wildlife Fund, https://www.worldwildlife.org

28. Fuel Freedom Foundation

29. Forest Declaration, https://www.forestdeclaration.org

30. Earth Overshoot

31. Global Footprint Network

32. Minister of Environment, Eugenie Sage, Stuff, 4 May 2018

33. Recycle New Zealand

34. Green Palm, https://www.greenpalm.org

35. The Guardian, 28 September 2017, Rainforest Action Network

36. Healthline, Alina Petre, 17 December 2018

37. Journal of Environmental and Public Health

38. Bisphenol-A Fact Sheet by the Centers for Disease Control and Prevention

39. Ecowatch. Earth Day Network

40. National Geographic

41. Ministry of the Environment, Japanese Agency. Estimated Total Amount of Debris Washed Out by the Great East Japan Earthquake. http://www.env.go.jp/en/focus/docs/files/20120901-57.pdf.(2012)

42. J.R. Jambeck, R. Geyer, C. Wilcox, T.R. Siegler, M. Perryman, A. Andrady, R. Nara, K.L. Law, Plastic waste inputs from land into ocean. Science, 347 (6223) (2015),pp.768-771

43. National Geographic, 28 February 2019, Laura Parker and Sarah Gibbons

44. University of Exeter. Marine turtles dying after becoming entangled in plastic rubbish. Science Daily, 18 December 2017

45. The Guardian, 22 March 2018

Chapter 12

1. Science Questions with Surprising Answers, Dr. Christopher S. Baird, When will the written word become obsolete? 31 May 2013, West Texas A & M University, wtamu.edu